FIGHTING THE GOOD FIGHT

The Life and Work of Benajah Harvey Carroll

The most popular photograph of B. H. Carroll.
— Courtesy Southwestern Baptist Theological Seminary Archives

FIGHTING THE GOOD FIGHT

The Life and Work of Benajah Harvey Carroll

By

Alan J. Lefever

EAKIN PRESS ⬧ Fort Worth, Texas
www.EakinPress.com

Special Edition

Copyright © 1994
By Alan J. Lefever
Published By Eakin Press
An Imprint of Wild Horse Media Group
P.O. Box 331779
Fort Worth, Texas 76163
1-817-344-7036
www.EakinPress.com
ALL RIGHTS RESERVED
1 2 3 4 5 6 7 8 9
ISBN-10: 1-940130-62-X
ISBN-13: 978-1-940130-62-X

Library of Congress Cataloging-in-Publication Data

Lefever, Alan J.
    Fighting the good fight : the life and work of Benajah Harvey Carroll / by Alan J. Lefever. — 1st ed.
        p.   cm.
    Includes bibliographical references and index.
    ISBN 978-1-940130-62-0
    1. Carroll, B. H. (Benajah Harvey), 1843–1914. 2. Southern Baptist Convention — Texas — Clergy — Biography. 3. Baptists — Texas — Clergy — Biography. 4. Southwestern Baptist Theological Seminary — History. 5. Texas — Biography. I. Title.
BX6495.C33L44   1994
286´.1´092--dc20
    [B]   93-44797
                                                                              CIP

To my parents

Walter and Jacqueline Lefever

*who started me down the
road of life
and my wife*

Sara

*who now walks with me
along the way.*

Contents

Foreword

B. H. Carroll's life and ministry encompassed a sweeping landscape marked by "mountainous" causes such as the Civil War, spiritual conversion, local church ministry, social action, denominational leadership, doctrinal controversy, and university education. Therefore it is appropriate that Alan J. Lefever's biography devotes most of its pages to these issues and only one-fifth of its pages to Carroll's strategic involvement with Southwestern Baptist Theological Seminary. It is difficult, however, for those of us presently engaged in the work of the institution he founded, to see him from any other perspective than the seminary.

So while others, for a variety of reasons, will benefit from this carefully researched and lucidly written story, those of us at Southwestern will read the book for its valuable insights for current theological education. It shows us how as the president, Carroll handled controversy, how he found time both for academics and administration, how he balanced theoretical learning with practice, and how he defended doctrinal orthodoxy without sacrificing the Baptist ideal of "the priesthood of believers." Since these issues are still on the agenda of ministry training today, we seminarians should be excused for this focused reading.

A number of articles are available on the life and work of Carroll along with numerous brief accounts of his ministry given in "Founders Day Addresses" at Southwestern and two early biographies by J. B. Cranfill and J. M. Carroll. But, unlike these accounts that often read like sentimental memorials, Lefever's effort is an historian's objective analysis based on extensive research. He shares new insights about Carroll that have not been widely known, treats with candor the less than complimentary events in his life, and thereby provides the reader with a realistic portrait.

Furthermore, the author has attempted to reach behind the historical data to try to understand and reconstruct the person of B. H.

Carroll. After reading the book, one feels a sense of personal acquaintance with the Texas giant. The author's frank and impartial approach does not obscure his sensitive appreciation for B. H. Carroll's greatness.

As the fifth president of Southwestern since B. H. Carroll's death, I have a unique personal appreciation for this story. B. H. Carroll becomes for me a model of enormous proportions for the office I now hold. He represents the priceless heritage that shapes and nurtures Southwestern, and he reminds us of the awesome responsibility we have to preserve for the future the institution he founded. We are inspired by B. H. Carroll's single-minded commitment without which, Alan Lefever reminds us, "Southwestern Seminary would not have become a reality, nor would his life and work have been ensconced in the pantheon of Baptist leaders."

RUSSELL H. DILDAY
President
Southwestern Baptist Theological Seminary

Preface

The life of Benajah Harvey Carroll has been an intriguing subject for me from my arrival in Waco as a freshman at Baylor University. While on staff at First Baptist Church, Waco, I read some of the church minutes written during Carroll's pastorate and began to wonder what Carroll must have been like as both a person and a pastor. After preaching occasionally at First Baptist, I often wondered what it must have been like to hear Carroll preach from the same pulpit.

Upon becoming the research assistant in the Archives of Southwestern Seminary during my second year as an M.Div. student, I became aware of the more than eight hundred folders comprising the personal papers of Carroll which are housed in Archives. During my spare time (and sometimes during work), I often read through Carroll's papers, obtaining small glimpses into this unique man. After entering the Ph.D. program, I asked Dr. H. Leon McBeth about the possibility of doing a biographical study on Carroll for my dissertation. His response was positive. The dissertation which resulted from his encouragement is the basis for this work.

As with any biographical study, not all of the events in Carroll's life are found in this book. Although he was not the superhuman minister that both his brother J. M. and his former student Jeff D. Ray present in their works, he was nevertheless an amazing character in Baptist history and a leader from a small boy until his death. Each day, whether they realize it or not, the students and faculty of Southwestern Seminary are touched by Carroll's life and work.

One never completes a book alone. There are many people who have contributed, both knowing and unknowing, to its completion whom I would like to thank. I have been fortunate throughout my education to have had history teachers who have made the subject come alive for me, thus pointing me in the direction that my life has now taken. In particular I would like to thank Sherry McKinney

Goss, Paul Armistead, and H. Leon McBeth, whose approaches to interpreting history helped to mold my own.

I would also like to thank Herbert H. Reynolds, president of Baylor University, and Russell H. Dilday, president of Southwestern Seminary, for allowing me access to the Board of Trustees minutes from their respective schools. The First Baptist Church of Waco also greatly aided my work by allowing me to use their original church minutes in my research. In addition I would like to thank the following: Ben Rogers, former Archivist at Southwestern, for hiring me many years ago and pointing me in the right direction in my Carroll research; Dr. Carl R. Wrotenbery, Director of Libraries at Southwestern, for his assistance in allowing me to complete this work quickly; Kent Keeth and Ellen Brown, of the Texas Collection at Baylor University, for providing related material from the Collection for my use; my Ph.D. colleagues, especially Karen Bullock, Glenn Carson, and Steve Stookey, who have learned more about Carroll than they ever wanted to know; Naomi Harmon, my secretary, and Arlette Coumbs, my archival assistant, whose help has been invaluable; and Jill Wiggins, my former secretary, who typed much of the final draft of this work.

Finally I would like to thank my mother and father, Jacqueline and Walter Lefever, who instilled in me from the earliest days of my childhood the confidence that I would need to complete this book. Thanks also go to my wife's parents, Jane and Clement Goode, who answered numerous questions on grammar and form. And my gratitude can never adequately be expressed for my wife, Sara, who for eight years has labored over my handwritten pages, turning them into respectable, academic papers.

Introduction

In every era of Baptist history, leaders have emerged who have become navigators of the faith through their beliefs and actions. These men serve as guides to their fellow Baptists, attempting to teach them the proper religious course. Yet these men not only guide their contemporaries, they also set a course which future Baptists will follow. In the latter half of the nineteenth century, Benajah Harvey Carroll emerged to become one of the navigators of this era, whose greatest navigational tool would be the founding of Southwestern Baptist Theological Seminary. Contemporaries of Carroll felt confident that history would recognize and record the importance of this man. J. B. Cranfill, in what now seems an almost prophetic statement, said:

> When current history shall have become archives and when the stately figure of B. H. Carroll shall outline itself against the background of time, the world will then know that in our own day, touching elbows with us, sacrificing for us, laboring with us, and giving to us of his time, energies, zeal, strength, power and leadership, none loomed larger in the life of the great Christian world.[1]

In 1865 much of the southern United States lay in ruin. Out of the ashes of these times, B. H. Carroll emerged to become one of the most prominent Southern Baptists of his era. Carroll, like many Southern men, had fought in the Civil War and had been wounded not only physically but emotionally. Searching for tranquility, he decided to experiment with the Christianity that his parents strongly believed in. The result was the beginning of almost fifty years of Christian faith and service.

When Carroll began his ministry in 1866, Texas had been a member of the United States for only twenty-one years. She was then, and would be for many years to come, part of the frontier.

Baptist work in Texas was older than the state itself. Since Joseph Bays preached the first Baptist sermon on Texas soil in 1820, Texas Baptists had formed associations, had organized statewide bodies, and had established two Baptist universities. The conversion of Texas legend Sam Houston was an early sign of the influence of Baptists in the state. Though early Baptist work in Texas had experienced success, many challenges remained that would be addressed during the latter half of the nineteenth century. This time became an age of conflict for Texas Baptists both inside and outside of the denomination. Carroll was only just beginning his role as a minister, but he was already a veteran fighter who loved conflict. Using his skills as a debater and orator, he quickly became the champion of the Baptist cause.

Carroll had a leading role in addressing all major Texas Baptist controversies of his day. His interests and talents, however, were not confined to controversy. Carroll was an active and effective pastor at the local church level and was a dominant figure in Texas Baptist mission work and education as well. As Baptist work in Texas matured, so too did Carroll. By the 1880s his leadership was no longer limited to Texas, as he began to have an influence on Baptist work throughout the South. Carroll's impact on Southern Baptist work was so great during the latter half of his ministry that at the time of his death he was called one of the greatest Southern Baptists who had ever lived.

After Carroll's death, many of his contemporaries wanted to record the significant events of his life in an effort to preserve his contributions for future generations. These early biographers quickly admitted a bias when approaching the life and work of Carroll. Their works resemble long eulogies rather than biographies. The mere power of Carroll's personality made objective studies by men who knew him virtually impossible. While they recorded his actions, they never examined his motives beyond the cause that he was leading.

Like the early biographers, this author will record the life and work of B. H. Carroll and show the important role that he played in Baptist history. Unlike the earlier works, however, this study will not only acknowledge Carroll's great contributions but will reveal the man behind those contributions as well. This in-depth examination of Carroll will review his early life to show the impact that it had on the rest of his ministry, will examine his beginnings as a minister and denominational activist, will highlight Carroll's maturation into a leader and spokesman for Baptists not only in Texas but throughout the Southern Baptist Convention, and will study Carroll's actions in light of his reactions and motives as well as the impact that each action had on Baptist work.

The work will conclude with a look at what many believe to be Carroll's greatest contribution to Southern Baptist life—the founding of Southwestern Baptist Theological Seminary. Tracing a course from Carroll's early involvement in ministerial education to his laying of the groundwork for the seminary at Baylor University to his founding of the seminary in Fort Worth, this work will go beyond a mere overview of the subject in order to examine Carroll's motives for creating a new seminary and his beliefs concerning the purpose of a seminary.

This biography on the life and work of B. H. Carroll should not be seen as an attempt to second-guess Carroll or to belittle his accomplishments. It should instead serve as a reminder that Christian history is made up of faithful but imperfect men and women who, through their life and work, attempt to carry out the will of God as they understand it.

Members of Carroll family, left to right: B. H. Carroll, E. B. Carroll, Laban Carroll, J. L. Carroll, J. M. Carroll.
     — Courtesy Southwestern Baptist Theological Seminary Archives

CHAPTER 1

Early Life

BOYHOOD

Benajah Harvey (B. H.) Carroll was born in Carroll County, Mississippi, on December 27, 1843. He was the seventh of twelve children born to Benajah and Mary Eliza Carroll. In addition to their own children, the Carrolls also reared twelve adopted orphans.[1] At the age of seven, in late 1850 or early 1851, B. H. moved with his family to Drew County, Arkansas, where he would spend the next eight years.[2] Little information exists on B. H.'s life during this period, though apparently it was the typical frontier life of a boy at the time: days filled with work on the farm and free time for fishing, hunting, and other "boyhood sports."[3]

James Milton (J. M.) Carroll, B. H.'s younger brother, records one incident that occurred during this time that illustrates the "bent of his [B. H.'s] mind and the trend of his life." One night after B. H. and several other boys in the area had been hunting, they paused to "tell tales" near a deserted house that was believed to be haunted. Soon the boys began daring one another to enter the house with the promise of a reward to anyone who would go in. J. M. records that B. H., who had never been afraid of "darkness, loneliness nor spooks of any sort," accepted their dare to enter the house for the reward of all the "strings, tops, marbles and barlow-knifes" that the boys had in their pockets. B. H. apparently stayed inside longer than

1

the boys had expected, for they were about to flee when he finally emerged. With their knees trembling and their hearts beating rapidly, the boys asked B. H. what he had seen. In response B. H. stated: "The thing that I saw was better than God and worse than the devil: dead men live on it: but if live men eat it they die." J. M. notes that this answer did nothing to relieve the fears of the boys and concludes that one can only guess what B. H. really saw.[4]

This story indicates that early in B. H.'s life he understood the power of manipulation. If he had returned saying that the house was old and empty, his adventure quickly would have been forgotten. By responding with the answer that he did, however, B. H. kept the boys' fear of the house alive and acquired respect for himself for accomplishing something that none of the other boys had done in the past nor would probably do in the future. This incident also reveals a trait that can be seen throughout B. H.'s life — he never walked away from a challenge.

In 1858 the family moved on, settling in Burleson County, Texas. During the long trip B. H. spent his days reading while he rode slightly ahead of the family on his mule. In fact, the day that the family arrived in Burleson County, B. H. got lost because his mule took a wrong road while B. H. was reading. When the family noticed that he had not arrived with them, they sent out a search party. After realizing that he had become separated from his family, B. H. returned a few hours later.[5]

As a boy of fourteen, B. H. would again use fear to manipulate those around him. In an effort to scare the Carroll family slaves, B. H. dressed like a ghost as part of a prank. The plan worked, and many of the slaves ran from their camp into the woods out of fear.[6]

FAMILY

Jesse Carroll, the great-grandfather of B. H., came to America in the 1700s from Ireland. Though details of the family history in Ireland are sketchy, the Carroll family was well versed in its Irish roots.[7] Benajah, B. H.'s father, was born in Sampson County, North Carolina, in 1807. Standing six feet four inches tall and weighing 200 pounds, Benajah was a descendant of "physical giants." These physical characteristics would be passed on to his eight sons, whose average height was six feet three inches.[8]

After his marriage to Mary Eliza Mallard, his second wife, Benajah moved his family to Mississippi in 1840.[9] He provided for

B. H. Carroll (seated), J. M. Carroll (standing).
— Courtesy Southwestern Baptist Theological Seminary Archives

them by farming; however, like many men of his family he was also a
minister. Though he pastored many churches throughout his adult
life in Mississippi, Arkansas, and Texas, he received little compensa-
tion for this work.

J. M. Carroll doubted that his father was paid more than one
hundred dollars in any one year.[10]

Though the Carrolls lived on a meager farm income, according
to J. M. they owned "many" slaves. Benajah was "by nature a
fighter" and would often offer freedom to any of his slaves who
could beat him in a fight. No record exists of a slave ever "winning"
his freedom from Benajah in this manner.[11]

Benajah's love for fighting was not limited to contests with
slaves, as J. M. notes that no man could safely question his father's
honor.[12] B. H. obviously inherited this attitude; for he never let a
question of his own honor go unanswered, and he never ran away
from a fight. In fact, just like his father he seemed to enjoy a good
fight.

During the family's trip to Texas, J. M. records that his father
led the family in two firmly established "family customs," which
seemed to be "inconsistent and even contradictory" as well as dangerous — family prayers every night and the drinking of whiskey
every morning. In recalling the morning practice J. M. states:

> that morning custom, almost universal then, produced a terrible
> harvest of hard drinkers and even drunkards in the next genera-
> tion. . . . I am sorry to say it, but several of my brothers were later
> found in the awful harvest of hard drinkers. My brother B. H.
> came very nearly getting into that harvest. . . . Nothing but the
> grace and mercy of God in later years saved several of my brothers
> from a drunkard's life and a drunkard's death. So much for one of
> the "good old customs."[13]

B. H.'s role in the Prohibition Movement in his later years has a
new meaning when seen against this backdrop of his early exposure
to alcohol.

Soon after arriving in Texas, Benajah Carroll began pastoring a
Baptist church as he had done in Mississippi and Arkansas. On the
fourth Sunday of February 1859, Dove Baptist Church in Caldwell
called Benajah as pastor. The church had been founded in 1843 with
six charter members under the leadership of R. E. B. Baylor and
Noah T. Byars.[14]

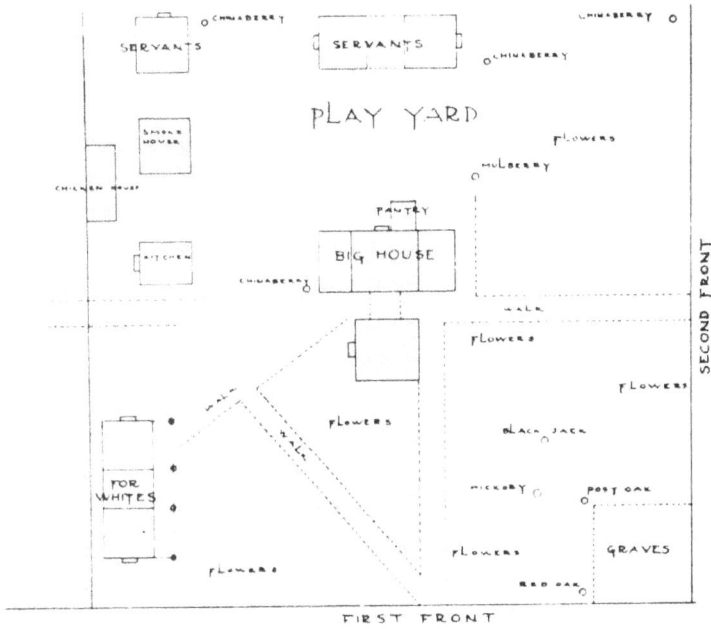

Plan of Old Carroll home site in 1858.
— Courtesy Southwestern Baptist Theological Seminary Archives

J. M. Carroll (right) and J. C. Hardy in front of the Old Carroll home.
— Courtesy Southwestern Baptist Theological Seminary Archives

When Benajah assumed the pastorate, Dove had a membership of 214 and was the largest church in the Little River Baptist Association. Benajah quickly rose to a leadership position within the association when it elected him moderator in September 1859 and appointed him to standing committees that were involved with the State Convention and ministerial education.[15] The following year the association reelected Benajah as moderator, and he delivered the meeting's introductory sermon from Hosea 4:6 entitled "The Duty of Churches is to Impart Instruction."[16]

Although Benajah was self-taught and had received no formal education, in his 1860 report concerning ministerial education he clearly recognized the need for a classical education as well as biblical study for the ministers of his day:

> A want of education has impeded the progress of the ministry of the word in every age of the world. . . . A desire to preach, even with the most pious, is not enough within itself to qualify for the ministerial office. Together with the necessary call to the ministry there must be an aptness to teach. . . . The uninformed and the partially informed are not apt to teach nor edify. A question here suggests itself in relation to the necessary qualifications of the ministery *[sic]*. We remark that a classical education is not only admissible, but highly desirable, nevertheless it will prove ineffectual without a knowledge of scripture. . . . In conclusion: Your committee believes that a biblical education is indispensable to the success of the ministry, and a proper training of the flock of Christ.[17]

As a representative of the association, Benajah traveled extensively during 1860 as a delegate to the state convention and as a corresponding messenger to the Union and San Marcos associational meetings.[18]

In the summer of 1861, soon after accepting a second pastorate, Benajah critically injured himself while attempting to mount a horse. The stirrup snapped, and Benajah's entire weight fell "upon the sharp horn of the saddle."[19] As a result of the accident, the Texas Rangers granted B. H. leave for a time to return to Caldwell to help his family. At the associational meeting in September 1861, the messengers took note of Benajah's condition in the following resolution:

> Whereas we have heard with deep feelings of regret that our much esteemed and worthy brother, Elder B. Carroll, now pastor of this (Cameron) church, and once the moderator of this association, is

suffering under the afflicting hand of Providence from a desease *[sic]* which may sooner or later terminate his earthly existence, and which does now paralize *[sic]* his usefulness as an able minister of the gospel. Resolved, that we offer our condolence to him in his afflictions, and our prayers to Almighty God for his delivery.[20]

Benajah was never able to recover from the fall. He died on March 9, 1862, in Caldwell.

B. H.'s mother, Mary Eliza, was a direct descendant of French Huguenots; her ancestors had come to America to flee the persecutions of their native France. She married Benajah on October 15, 1828, when she was sixteen. According to J. M. Carroll, Mary Eliza did a masterful job of running a house full of twenty-four children; and her strength alone kept the family together during the Civil War after the death of Benajah. In describing his mother, J. M. notes:

None of her twelve children patterned closely after her in size or color of hair (she had red hair), or sweetness of character. And yet the lives of all her eight boys and four girls were mightily influenced by her life and disposition. No storm of wrath, whether in the husband or any one or more of her firey-tempered *[sic]* children, could rage long in her presence. Oh, my Lord, what a mother! I dare not attempt to picture her further. The world would not and could not believe. Rest on now, little mother. Never woman lived more gloriously nor to a higher, nobler and more successful end.[21]

Mary Eliza died at the age of fifty-seven in 1869. Except for a brief mention in his autobiographical sermon, "My Infidelity and What Became of It," B. H. recorded nothing of his relationship with his parents; yet their influence is undeniable. B. H.'s views on ministerial education and scripture had their foundation in the beliefs of his father. And the calming influence of his mother comforted B. H. during the confusing and trying event of his conversion.

RELIGIOUS LIFE

"My Infidelity and What Became of It" is also the only record of B. H.'s early religious life. B. H. noted that he grew up in a Christian home with a "self-educated minister" for a father and a "devoted Christian" for a mother. Even the teachers who instructed him were Christians. Yet something inside of B. H. left him skeptical of Christianity.[22]

This skepticism, or "doubt" as B. H. called it, appeared to come in waves, growing stronger as he matured. In recalling the growth of these doubts, B. H. wrote:

> From unremembered time this skepticism progressed irregularly. Sometimes in one hour there would be more progress in extent and definiteness than in previous months. These short periods of huge advances were always sudden and startling. Place and circumstances had but little to do with them. The doubt was seldom germane to the topic under consideration. At times it came when I was in the Sunday School or hearing a sermon or bowed with the others in family prayer — more frequently when waking at night after healthful sleep, and still more frequently when rambling alone in the fields or woods, or mountain heights.[23]

Although doubts about Christianity raged within B. H., the people around him apparently were unaware of his struggle. When B. H. was thirteen a protracted meeting was held in his community which resulted in many people joining the church and being baptized. B. H. stated that many of these conversions were genuine; however, he believed that others were a product of people simply going "with the tide." During one of the meetings which B. H. attended — because it was a "curious spectacle" — two men approached him and asked three questions concerning scripture, Jesus, and salvation. After B. H. answered all of the questions in the affirmative, the men presented him before the preachers of the meeting for baptism and church membership.[24]

According to B. H.'s recollection of the event, he had no idea that his mechanical answers would be seen as a sign of conversion because he was not converted. If the practice had been followed of having all who came for baptism and membership give a testimony of their experience, B. H. believed that he would have been discovered as unconverted, for he had no testimony. Many had joined, however; and because of the lateness of the hour, the church accepted B. H. for baptism and membership without his having to speak.[25]

In recalling this event, B. H. noted three problems. First, the church workers who questioned him were overly zealous. Second, his answers were historical "as if from a textbook." Third, he was only thirteen. In other words, if the men had taken time to notice the shallowness of his answers as well as his youth, they would have realized that B. H. was unconverted.[26] The third statement by B. H. concerning his age indicates that he may have had reservations about the conversion of children.

Ironically, B. H.'s baptism led him to an awareness of his own infidelity:

> Walking home from the baptism the revelation came. The vague infidelity of all the past took positive shape, and would not down at my bidding. My answers had been educational. I did not believe that the Bible was God's revelation. I did not believe in miracles or the divinity or vicarious sufferings of Jesus. I had no confidence in conversion and regeneration. There was no perceptible change in my disposition or affections. What I once loved, I still loved; what I once hated, I still hated. It was no temporary depression as sometimes comes to genuine Christians.
>
> Joining the church, with its assumption of obligations, acted on me like the touch of Ithuriel's spear. I saw my real self. I know that either I had no religion or it was not worth having. The sensation of actual and positive infidelity was so new to me that I hardly knew what to say about it. I felt a repugnance to parade it. I wanted time and trial for its verification. I knew that its avowal would pain and horrify my family and the church, yet honesty required me to say something.[27]

B. H. asked the church to withdraw his membership on the grounds that he was unconverted. The church, believing B. H.'s feelings to be temporary, advised him to read his Bible and pray. So B.H. read his Bible as "never before," but still he found no peace on "contradictions and fallacies." Although his doubts remained strong, when B. H.'s family moved to Texas he decided to retain his membership while he continued to study.[28]

In reflecting upon his early religious life, B. H. clearly recognized that while he was an infidel he was far from being an atheist:

> I know now that I never doubted the being, personality and government of God. I was never an atheist or pantheist. I never doubted the existence and ministry of angels — pure spirits never embodied: I could never have been a Sadducee. I never doubted the essential distinction between spirit and matter: I could never have been a materialist.[29]

EDUCATION

The extent of B. H.'s education before his arrival in Texas is impossible to determine, though clearly he was able to read and write. Soon after arriving B. H., along with his brothers, began to

R. C. Burleson, president of Baylor University 1851–61, 1886–97; Waco University 1861–86.

— Courtesy Southwestern Baptist Theological Seminary Archives

Artist's conception of Baylor University at Independence about 1850s.
— Courtesy Baylor University Texas Collection

View of Independence from the Baylor University Campus.
— Courtesy Baylor University Texas Collection

attend school in the town of Caldwell. After six months T. K. Crittenden, his teacher, told B. H.: "I cannot teach you any further; you know more than I do. You will be compelled to go elsewhere." Therefore, in the fall of 1859, at the age of sixteen, B. H. enrolled in a small Baptist school thirty miles from Caldwell known as Baylor University. Because of his prior education and knowledge, Baylor admitted him as a full junior.[30]

While at Baylor B. H. began a strong and long-lasting friendship with Rufus C. Burleson, president of Baylor. B. H. quickly impressed Burleson with his speaking and debating skills. Robert A. Baker believes that B. H. probably arrived on the campus of Baylor with a reputation as an outstanding debater from debates held in Caldwell:

> One of the favorite stories around Caldwell related how Carroll took the affirmative side of the question of whether the followers of Alexander Campbell were right in their doctrines. He won the debate. He then promptly took the negative side and won that also. This suggests the precocity of the sixteen-year-old boy who was not at that time religiously inclined.[31]

During his days at Baylor, B. H. debated twice a week. The zeal with which he could defend a position that he did not fully believe in would prove to be an ominous sign for those who would later debate him over positions to which he was fully committed.

Like his father, B. H. was a strong Unionist. In perhaps the greatest debate of his college career, Carroll was chosen to represent the affirmative at a town meeting discussing whether Texas should remain in the Union. Though the crowd was against his position at the beginning of the debate, after his speech, which one witness stated "stirred this old historic town of Independence as no other speech in its history ever stirred it," the crowd enthusiastically raised the Union flag on a pole. Their mood changed overnight, however, and the next day the crowd, led by the mayor, cut the pole down and dragged the flag through the dust.[32]

With the secession of Texas, B. H. left Baylor before taking his final examinations in order to join the Texas Rangers in guarding the Texas frontier. While other Baylor men who joined the Rangers and the regular army were granted their degrees, B. H. apparently was not. B. H.'s enlistment in the Rangers ended his formal education, although he would continue to be a scholar throughout his life.[33]

THE CIVIL WAR

B. H. Carroll strongly believed in the Union and, according to his brother, would have preferred fighting for the Union; but he joined a regiment of Rangers, along with some of his brothers, to protect the Texas frontier. He was mustered into the Confederate service in San Antonio on April 15, 1861.[34]

The mission of the Texas Rangers in 1861 was to help stabilize the frontier and to establish Confederate control over forts held by Union forces. This period was an exciting time for the young Carroll. In reviewing Carroll's time as a Ranger, J. M. states:

> The forts were soon all captured. Then followed a long period of cavalry scouting, some Indian chasing, intermingled with frequent fishing, turkey, deer, buffalo, and other large game hunting. The Indians were always wary while the soldiers were around. This regiment, however, was trained and used more as rangers than as soldiers. The Indians feared the rangers more than they did the soldiers.[35]

Though Carroll was a mature young adult, he still enjoyed a good prank. One day a new recruit asked to witness Texas Ranger marksmanship. Carroll, who according to his brother was "never a great shot," stepped forward to show the recruit what he could do with his gun. Shooting into a covey of prairie chickens, Carroll miraculously shot the head off a big hen. When the young man asked Carroll if he always shot that way, Carroll replied: "Do you think we would mar our game by shooting these chickens anywhere else but in the head?" Impressed with this display of shooting, the recruit asked Carroll to shoot the head gander in a flock of geese flying by. Undaunted by this second request, Carroll raised his rifle and fired with, as J. M. records, "the amazing and miraculous result that by the purest accident imaginable he [Carroll] brought down the head gander and had shot him at the juncture of the head and neck." When the young recruit brought the bird to Carroll, Carroll became upset, complaining: "I shot this gander an eighth of an inch too far back."[36]

The adventure of the frontier soon ended for Carroll. In the fall of 1861 he received word that his father had been seriously injured in a riding accident. As a result, B. H. and one of his brothers returned to Caldwell in November 1861, on furlough from the Rangers.

THE "GREAT TRAGEDY"

A major event occurred in Carroll's life at this time, one which would haunt him for the rest of his life. Neither J. M. Carroll nor J. B. Cranfill mention it at all in their works concerning Carroll, and Jeff D. Ray merely remarks:

> Then came his life's great tragedy. I shall not describe it further than to say that I lived four years in the community where it occurred and I know that everybody there acquitted him of blame in the tragic transaction, and there was no spot on earth where he was more honored and trusted than in that community.[37]

Though Ray does not name the event, he clearly states that no one held Carroll responsible for it. What, in fact, was this "great tragedy"? On December 13, 1861, Carroll married Ophelia A. Crunk while he was home on furlough from the Rangers. Carroll was eighteen at the time, and Ophelia was fifteen. The Crunk and Carroll families had apparently known each other for some time; however, little is known of how well Ophelia and B. H. knew each other prior to this contact and marriage in 1861.[38]

When Carroll had to return to the Rangers two weeks after the wedding, Ophelia refused to join him. When Carroll asked her why she would not live with him, her only reported reason was that she did not love him. Carroll returned to the army, leaving Ophelia in Caldwell. Three months later he came to Caldwell to try once again to persuade Ophelia to join him. Again he was unsuccessful. Although she refused to join him, she had apparently remained faithful to her wedding vows. This faithfulness would soon end.[39]

In 1863, while Carroll was with the Confederate Army in Louisiana, one of his brothers, with Carroll's consent, sued for a divorce on the grounds of adultery. R. E. B. Baylor presided over the divorce trial, which was heard by a jury. Ophelia did not deny the charge of adultery, and the court granted the divorce on November 9, 1863; Ophelia paid all court costs.[40] Burleson County records show that two days later, on November 11, 1863, Ophelia married B. D. Evans.[41] Although the hearing cleared Carroll of any wrongdoing in the divorce, this tragic event shattered his life, leaving him with little reason to live. In recalling the event nearly thirty years later, he stated:

> The battle of life was lost. In seeking the field of war I sought death. By peremptory demand I had my church connection dis-

solved, and turned utterly away from every semblance of Bible belief. In the hour of my darkness I turned unreservedly to infidelity. This time I brought it a broken heart and a disappointed life, asking for light and peace and rest.[42]

THE BATTLE OF MANSFIELD

Devastated by the death of his father, as well as his second failed attempt to convince Ophelia to join him in West Texas, Carroll had transferred to the regular Confederate Army, which assigned him to the Seventeenth Regiment of the Texas Infantry.[43] If a young man wanted to turn "unreservedly to infidelity" in the early 1860s, there was no better place for such activity than the Confederate Army.

With the outbreak of war in 1861, the Confederate government moved quickly to institute a draft to help in raising troops. Not all who were drafted had to serve — the draftee could hire a substitute for $1,000. Since only the wealthy could afford such a fee, this practice produced the bitter slogan "rich man's war and poor man's fight."[44] As a result of this system almost ninety percent of the Confederate Army was composed of the poor or blue-collar men.[45]

As these men began to assemble throughout the South, Christians quickly called the moral integrity of the Confederate forces into question. Many felt the army camps were causing a great moral decline among the young soldiers living there. Vices available in the Confederate camps seduced these youg men who were free, often for the first time, from the restrictions of family and community. William W. Bennett believes that the greatest "evils" faced by the Southern soldiers were lewdness, profanity, and drunkenness.[46] Though few details exist concerning Carroll's activity in the Confederate Army, assuredly he did not spend all of his time on "infidelities" as he stated.

According to accounts of people who served with Carroll in the army, none was aware of the dark and deadly battle that "raged" within Carroll at this time.[47] Recalling their time together during this period, one such comrade, Woodson Patrick, stated:

he [Carroll] was a fine Robust young chaps as you would find anywhere and seemed to be a boiling over with energy. On our march from Austin to Little Rock he was at his best with his boyish pranks. Well he enlivened our camp fire sides all the way on that long and sore footed march when we wanted.[48]

During his time in the army, Carroll continued to polish his skills in debate and oration. J. M. notes that Carroll had little trouble finding opponents, as he always took the unpopular side. For example, in Arkansas, Carroll delivered a speech entitled "Delusions of the South" which explained why the South would be defeated. Later he delivered speeches discussing the plight of the Confederacy, such as "Effect of the Fall of Vicksburg" and "Resolved, That Confederate success is more to be dreaded than their defeat."[49]

While Carroll obviously enjoyed debating the current plight of the South, he did not limit his debates or speeches to politics alone. He also found religion to be worthy of discussion, and he began to debate the preachers who ministered to the Confederate troops. J. M. states:

> It was not an unusual thing for him, while in the army, to mount a stump or log and reply to the preachers who preached to the soldiers. More especially was this true if the preacher happened to have any vagaries. He thoroughly knew orthodoxy. . . . No wonder all preachers dreaded him.[50]

In describing Carroll's style of delivery, Patrick noted that Carroll "could make a Negro preacher ashamed of himself."[51]

Carroll did not spend all of his time in the army in debate and speechmaking, for he was a soldier as well. In recalling Carroll's service in later years, a colonel with whom Carroll had served wrote that Carroll was "a gallant soldier, always on the firing line and behaving with marked courage."[52] Perhaps in an effort to hasten his own death during this dark period of his life, Carroll often volunteered for the most dangerous missions. At the Battle of Milliken's Bend, Carroll led the charge against the Union defenses, not only miraculously escaping death at the hands of the enemy but avoiding being shot in the back by his own troops as well.[53]

On April 8, 1864, Carroll's good fortune ended. At the Battle of Mansfield a minnie ball, a large bullet used by Union forces, pierced his thigh and passed between the bone and the femoral artery. J. M. notes that given the crude surgery of the day, a "hair breath variation" in the trajectory of the bullet would have meant certain death. Carroll's brother Laban, who was fighting close to Carroll during the battle, picked him up and carried him for two miles until they were clear of the battlefield. In recording this event J. M. writes:

At one point the bullets were falling so thick and fast that Laban laid him down in a depression of the ground and waited a while. But the wounded boy was mad and desperate. He raised himself upon his elbow and cursed the Yankees, the brother begging him to lie down and hush, and protect himself. Finally, seeing that he would not try to protect himself, the strong and loving brother took him again in his arms and carried him as rapidly as possible off the battlefield. He carried him finally, by permission of his officers, to a little Southern cottage home where the generous people took them in, and there the one brother nursed the other through the long days while life hung upon a very brittle thread.[54]

In an effort to avoid worrying his mother, Carroll persuaded the war correspondent to record that he was only "slightly wounded." Most men wounded by a minnie ball eventually died from the wound.[55] Carroll survived, although he would suffer the effects of this injury for the rest of his life.

CAMP MEETING AND CONVERSION

As soon as Carroll was able, he returned to Caldwell to complete his recovery. He began teaching school in a small community known as Yellow Prairie, five miles from his home.[56] Though the physical war was now over for Carroll, a personal, spiritual battle which had been raging for many years continued.

A prayer written on April 10, 1864, reportedly attributed to Carroll, reveals that his search for truth and peace, and the role of Christianity in both, took on new importance after his injury at Mansfield. In the prayer Carroll pled:

> Therefore I ask in supplant tone,
> By hope that's lost and miseries known
> Is Jesus Christ, our Lord, thy Son?
> Reveal this hidden mystery.[57]

Though the "mystery" was not immediately revealed to him, his failure to find peace through philosophy was:

> Why had I never seen it before: These philosophies were mere negations; they overturned but built up nothing. I say nothing; I mean nothing. To the unstricken, curious soul, they are as beautiful as the aurora borealis, shining on arctic icebergs. But to me they warmed and melted nothing. No flowers bloomed and no fruit ripened under their cheerless beams. They looked down on

my bleeding heart as the cold, distant, pitiless stars have ever looked down on all human suffering. Whoever, in his hour of real need, rests on abstract philosophy, makes cold, hard granite his pillow. Whoever looks trustingly into its false faces, looks into the face of Medusa, and is turned to stone. They are all wells without water, and clouds without rain in a parching drouth.[58]

As Carroll's body began to heal, his heart once again hardened to the gospel. When he was twenty-two he decided never to enter a church again.

His mother persuaded him to attend a Methodist camp meeting with her one morning in the fall of 1865. Although the sermon left Carroll unmoved, the plea of the preacher at the end of the service seemed to be personalized for him:

You that stand aloof from Christianity and scorn us simple folks, what have you got? . . . if there be a God, mustn't there be a something somewhere? If so, how do you know it is not here? Are you willing to test it? I don't ask you to read any book, nor study any evidences, nor make any pilgrimages. Are you willing to try it now; to make a practical, experimental test, you to be the judge of the result?[59]

This experiment sounded interesting to Carroll, who was leaning on his crutches at the back of the group; and he decided to give it a try. When he went forward at the close of the meeting, Carroll was not prepared for the response that his action would bring as the crowd shouted its approval. To quiet the joyous group, Carroll quickly stated that he had not been converted but was only conducting an "experimental test" of Christianity.[60]

Carroll, along with his brother J. M., returned to the evening service, where J. M. remembered the preacher's final plea to Carroll to give his heart to God before he left.[61] Carroll went forward again, this time obviously moved by the message. Yet with tears rolling down his face, he still refused to make a public stand for Christianity. While Carroll seemed ready to make a decision; he refused to be swayed by the emotion of the moment until he was absolutely certain that the decision being made was his. Thus Carroll's pride, a facet of his character which is prevalent throughout his life, prevented him from making a public profession that night.

After arriving home from the meeting, Carroll realized through a conversation with his mother that he had indeed "found the Lord":

I spent the night at her bedside reading *Pilgrim's Progress*. When I came with the pilgrims to the Beulah land, from which Doubting Castle could be seen no more forever, and which was within sight of the Heavenly City and within sound of the heavenly music, my soul was filled with a rapture and ecstacy *[sic]* of Joy such as I had never before experienced. I knew then as well as I know now, that I would preach; that it would be my life work; that I would have no other.[62]

A few days after Carroll's conversion experience, W. W. "Spurgeon" Harris, an old schoolmate and preacher, baptized Carroll. As Harris was neither pastoring the Caldwell church nor leading a revival in the area, the possibility exists that Carroll actually sent for his old friend to perform his baptism.[63] Carroll had been converted. Now this young man, whose activities had ranged from fighting, to playing pranks, to reading scholarly books, would use his energy, mind, and gift of oration to define and spread the Christian faith as he understood it.

CHAPTER 2

The Young Minister

Carroll's conversion experience not only included a profession of faith but also an acceptance of God's call to the ministry. The Caldwell Church, where he had asked only a year earlier to have his name removed from the rolls, first nominated him to positions of leadership within the church and then, on the fourth Sunday in May 1866, licensed Carroll to preach.[1] In June the church sent him as a messenger to a Sunday School convention. And by July it had appointed Carroll to serve as moderator at a church conference. Finally, on November 15, 1866, Caldwell ordained Carroll to the ministry. In recalling the ordination a few months later, J. S. Allen, one of the members of the presbytery, stated: "Brother Carroll, who is an excellent preacher and well qualified for his work, was ordained. A church that wants such a man would do well to call him from the schoolroom to his appropriate work."[2]

ELLEN BELL

For a brief period in 1866, Carroll taught school and pastored the Caldwell Church simultaneously.[3] During this time he married Ellen Bell, with whom he ministered for the next thirty years.

The Bell family had moved to Caldwell at the end of the Civil War. Ellen, according to J. M., was one of the "most attractive young women" in the town. Carroll apparently agreed with this assessment and became a frequent visitor to the Bell home. The time that Carroll spent with Ellen did not go unnoticed by her father. When asked where Carroll could be found on one occasion, her father, an avid deer hunter, remarked: "I don't know where he is just now, but if you will go, take a stand at my gate I think you will soon get a shot."[4]

Ellen was a strong and independent woman. Reared a Methodist, she became a Baptist after her marriage to Carroll. Ellen insisted that this decision was not made because of her husband's position as a Baptist minister but because she believed that Baptists were right on points that differentiated the two denominations. Ellen did disagree, however, with the Baptist view of apostasy. She believed throughout most of her life that a believer could "fall from grace," although according to Jeff Ray she "abandoned this view before her death."[5]

Ellen's independent nature is also seen in the way in which she filled her position as a "professional preacher's wife." Ellen saw her role as no different from that of any other woman in the church. Not only did she shun leadership positions in all women's organizations and aid societies within the church, but her overall participation in these groups was minimal. Her approach to the role of a preacher's wife, although unorthodox, was effective.

> Without display, and often secretly, she was an angel of blessing to the poor and needy and heart-sore in her husband's church and among her neighbors. The unfortunate, the heartbroken, the derelict from every walk of life turned instinctively to this sturdy, genuine woman for help, for comfort, for rejuvenation. . . . If there could pass before my reader at this moment all the people she helped he would witness a very long and a very motley parade.[6]

Ellen was devoted to Carroll and their nine children. Of the five who lived to adulthood, two were active in full-time Baptist work — Charles taught theology for many years at the Baptist Bible Institute in New Orleans, and Kate served as a missionary to Brazil. Ellen and Carroll were very different from each other; Ray states that "temperamentally they seemed poles apart." Yet they loved each other deeply. A young preacher once urged Carroll to attend Southern Seminary so that he could become a great preacher. Ellen asked the young man if he had attended Southern. When he answered in the affirmative, she quickly responded by saying: "Why didn't it make a great preacher of you?"[7]

EARLY MINISTRY

In 1867 the Carrolls' work unexpectedly moved to Post Oak, where Carroll had assisted S. G. O'Bryan in a revival during the previous summer. While returning home following the revival, O'Bryan became ill with yellow fever. The news spread quickly, and church members refused to aid O'Bryan for fear of catching the disease. Carroll, deciding to help, left the meeting and "went to the suffering preacher and nursed him until his death."[8] After O'Bryan's death, Carroll returned to the church and preached a sermon entitled "He Being Dead Yet Speaketh." As a result a great revival ensued. At the conclusion of the meeting the church, who had been impressed with the young preacher, offered to help him settle in the community and to pay him $800 a year. He, in turn, would teach in their literary school and become their pastor, preaching two Sundays a month.[9]

The Carrolls moved to Post Oak in the fall of 1867. For the next year and a half Carroll served Post Oak as well as other churches in the area. But the Carrolls found it impossible to exist on the money that they received from churches who were accustomed to their ministers working for virtually nothing. When Carroll resigned his pastorate and closed his school at Post Oak, he noted that the $800 promised him had not been paid; and if not for the gifts of two church members, he and his family would have "starved long ago."[10] At this time Carroll felt the need to work full time as a minister, meaning he would have to leave his part-time churches and go elsewhere. The financial problems that young preachers faced can be seen in the recollection of Carroll's brother concerning a farewell service at another of Carroll's churches:

> He told them of his conviction as to his duty to give his whole service to the ministry. Then of his call to another field, then of his sorrow at leaving them, etc. At the conclusion of the service and the talk, he remarked that he really needed a little money for moving expenses, and as the church as yet had paid him nothing for his services, that now would be a very appropriate and opportune time to help him. In fact the only time, as he was to leave the next week. But nothing was paid. In fact, the brethren seemed really hurt that a question like this should have been forced upon the meeting when everybody was feeling so sad and solemn. But, as the preacher was young, they forgave him but they did not help him any financially.[11]

In 1868 Carroll conducted a revival at Spring Hill, about ten miles southeast of Waco. In reporting the revival in the *Texas Baptist Herald*, Carroll stated:

> We had a glorious time. The glory of God in conviction and conversion passed among the people in manifest power. There had been preaching in the neighborhood once a month, but no church organization, no warmth, no awakening of sinners. The meeting lasted several days and nights. A church was organized.[12]

The church that was organized as a result of this meeting was New Hope Baptist Church, which in 1869 invited Carroll to become its pastor. Unfortunately for the people at New Hope, Carroll's pastorate there was brief. Shortly after his arrival events were set into motion that led to Carroll's becoming pastor at First Baptist Church, Waco.[13]

CALL TO FIRST BAPTIST CHURCH, WACO

Traditionally historians have believed that Judge R. E. B. Baylor, for whom Baylor University is named, preached the first Baptist sermon in Waco during a court session in 1851. Noah T. Byars, however, a state missionary for the Southern Baptist Convention, had probably made at least one or two visits to the community before Judge Baylor.[14] Byars was instrumental in establishing the First Baptist Church of Waco, which was organized on May 31, 1851. The church had four charter members who extended a call to Byars to become their pastor on June 1.[15] He served the Waco church for one weekend a month and spent the remaining weekends pastoring other small churches in Central Texas. The congregation was given permission by the Methodists to use their meeting house for two Sundays a month; they did so until 1852, when they established their own structure near the Brazos River. Failing health forced Byars to retire in 1854.

S. G. O'Bryan became the church's first pastor to live on the field. Within a few months of arriving in Waco, he challenged his membership of fewer than thirty to erect a brick building. This building served as their meeting place until 1877, when it was destroyed by fire.[16] One of the highlights of O'Bryan's pastorate was the revival of September 1857, which resulted in seventy-four conversions, many of whom were prominent citizens of the community.[17] O'Bryan also played a major role in the development of the Waco Classical School, which later became Waco University and

eventually merged with Baylor University in 1886. After six successful and growing years at First Baptist, O'Bryan was not reelected in 1860 as the church felt that he was no longer the best man
for their pastorate.

Carroll, who obviously admired O'Bryan's work, as indicated
in a life sketch he wrote, nursed O'Bryan until his death in 1867.
Whether O'Bryan ever shared with Carroll his feelings about his
dismissal from First Baptist in 1859 is unknown. If he did, that
might help to explain the way that Carroll manipulated the church
from time to time by mentioning the possibility that he might leave
or by actually tendering his resignation. When the time came for
Carroll to leave the pastorate at First Baptist, the decision would
clearly be his rather than that of the church.

The next ten years (1860-1870) consisted of short pastorates,
with the church often turning to Rufus C. Burleson to guide it.
Burleson came to Waco in 1860 from Independence to assume the
presidency of the newly created Waco University. Therefore from
time to time during this decade, First Baptist had a bi-vocational
pastor, with Burleson serving as both pastor and president. No
doubt the lack of consistent pastoral leadership during this ten-year
period hindered the growth of the church.

CARROLL'S ARRIVAL

In 1870, only twenty years after the founding of Waco, the
population of the city had grown from around 100 to over 2,000.
The town had suffered severely during the Civil War as many of the
larger plantations in the area closed. With the help of the cattle industry, the community recovered rapidly. The Waco Suspension
Bridge, the longest single-span bridge in the world at that time, was
built in 1870, allowing commerce to cross easily the Brazos River.
With the help of the railroad Waco became a "hub city" by 1871, a
southern boom town that had successfully made the change from
cotton to cattle as the lifeblood of the economy.[18]

In 1870 First Baptist Church was still meeting in the building
that O'Bryan had challenged them to build in 1857. The structure
was a basic one, and pews consisted of planks laid on blocks or
logs.[19] When First Baptist became pastorless at the end of 1869, the
church requested that Burleson fill the pulpit as he had done in the
past. Burleson informed the church that his duties at Waco University would allow him to preach only two Sundays a month and sug-

gested that the church contact B. H. Carroll, the young pastor at New Hope who had recently led a revival at First Baptist, to fill the pulpit on the remaining two Sundays each month.

On January 5, 1870, the church voted to extend a call to B. H. Carroll "to assist the pastor." The minutes of January 12 state: "Elder B. H. Carroll, being present, accepted the call of the church to preach in conjunction with our pastor."[20] On the Sundays that Carroll did not preach at First Baptist, he continued to preach at New Hope. In October 1870, Burleson informed First Baptist that he wished to be relieved of his pastoral duties. Following this announcement the church extended a call to Carroll to become pastor for an indefinite period of time, thus ending the practice of electing the pastor annually. Carroll accepted; and in March 1871, he moved his family to Waco to become First Baptist's full-time pastor.[21]

THE YOUNG PREACHER

Although Carroll had surrendered to the ministry, J. M. notes that "the devil did not let him go without a struggle." Carroll's quick temper and inability to accept criticism followed him in his ministry. To illustrate his point, J. M. relates an event that occurred after Carroll's arrival in Waco. J. M. was in town visiting his brother when Carroll began to discuss a problem that he was having with his young sons fighting all of the time. Carroll stated that he "could not imagine where his boys got their fighting proclivities." As J. M. and Carroll continued their discussion, they boarded a streetcar. When Carroll placed his ticket in the box, it was immediately covered by another ticket. The driver, concluding that Carroll had not paid, accused him of such, and an argument ensued. The argument ended when the driver jumped from the streetcar and exchanged places with a driver from an oncoming streetcar. A now irate Carroll caught the driver, however, and refused to let him go until he had apologized. After the incident was over and Carroll had returned to his seat, J. M. had to choke back his laughter. In a moment Carroll broke the awkward silence: "I think I can see where my boys got some of their fighting proclivities."[22] In a town the size of Waco, news of this incident spread quickly, and during the rest of Carroll's ministry few publicly questioned his honor or integrity although they did challenge his opinions on various issues.

Z. N. Morrell, a chronicler of Texas Baptist history, makes

note of "B. H. Carroll, the rising man in Texas Ministry," while recalling a visit to Waco in 1872:

> He [Carroll] possessed an active and inquiring mind. . . . Tall in person, and commanding in manner, he takes bold positions as a preacher, and is destined by the blessings of God with patient toil, to do valiant service on the battle ground of truth.[23]

Carroll's physical appearance in the pulpit was striking: six feet four inches tall, weighing 230 pounds, with auburn hair, a flowing beard, and steel gray eyes. He dominated the pulpit at First Baptist. Jeff D. Ray states that Carroll's gestures seemed to be set to music, and his voice, "though not always well controlled, was full of music and feeling, and, once heard, was never forgotten." Carroll had a commanding physical appearance throughout his ministry at First Baptist. Ray records the story of two Baylor students discussing Carroll. One stated that he was tired of Carroll's sermons because they were too long; the other replied: "I get tired of his sermons, too, but I never get tired of looking at him."[24]

Looking back on his early years at First Baptist, Carroll admitted that he had doubts about his ability to pastor the church because he was "young and inexperienced."[25] No record exists, however, of his ever letting this self-doubt show; and church minutes during his early ministry show that the congregation had full confidence in his leadership ability.

DEFENDER OF THE FAITH

Soon after Carroll began his full-time ministry at First Baptist, he had an opportunity to practice one of the skills that had brought him much pleasure throughout his young life — debating. In April 1871, a Methodist minister by the name of O. Fisher preached a series of sermons in Waco directed against Baptists. The *Texas Baptist Herald* outlined these sermons along with rejoinders by Carroll on behalf of the Baptist church in the May 10 issue. Following Fisher's sermons, members of First Baptist requested that Fisher agree to a debate on the issues or that he stop his attacks against the Baptists. He did neither. Fisher did agree to a joint meeting where he would speak and Carroll would reply.[26]

Evidence is unclear as to who was the victor of this joint meeting. Soon afterward, Fisher left Waco to continue his tour of Methodist churches in Texas. Fisher received word, however, that Carroll was calling himself the victor of their meeting. In a letter to Carroll dated May 31, 1871, Willis King stated:

> At the request of Rev. Dr. O. Fisher, this communication is addressed to you, the Doctor having learned, from what he regards as good authority, that you, while at Davilla, some time since, stated that you had beaten him in debate at Waco, and to such an extent as to drive him entirely from the arena of debate.[27]

In reply, Carroll denied making those statements. He said that he had only told a friend that he had answered Fisher's charge, thereby discrediting Fisher's claim that his challenge to the Baptists at Waco had gone unanswered. Carroll was willing to debate Fisher and agreed to meet him in Davilla on September 13, 1871, for that purpose.[28]

Though the debate occurred in September 1871, the *Texas Baptist Herald* printed the transcript as a series of articles from April 24 to October 16, 1872. In recalling the debate, A. J. Holt, who attended the event, states:

> The Methodists were especially jubilant, thinking that their favorite and famous champion would completely demolish this presumptuous young Baptist from Waco, that had dared to propose to meet in discussion, the far-famed Goliath of Methodism. The Baptists were fearful. B. H. Carroll was to them an unheard-of man.[29]

Holt continues his recollection of the event by giving his "unbiased" report of the results—the debate was a complete victory for the Baptists. He notes that even the Methodist judges had awarded the debate to Carroll. B. H. Carroll had become the Baptists' new champion; and like past champions, such as Alexander Campbell and J. R. Graves, many requested his services to help defend the faith. As a result of his surprising success, Carroll "gained great confidence in himself, in his positions, and in his brethren."[30] He chose not to become a debater for Baptists, however, but to return to Waco and to remain a minister of the Gospel. R. C. Buckner later stated that it was at the Davilla debate where Baptists realized that Carroll was a "giant among them."[31]

MUSIC AND MINISTRY

The portrayal of Carroll as a "defender of the faith" does not mean that he was a man locked into Baptist traditions. During his early years at First Baptist, Carroll was an innovator of Baptist practices. Perhaps the best two examples of this innovation are his ideas concerning church music and deacon ministry.

On February 5, 1873, at the regularly scheduled business meeting, church members "fully discussed" the "subject of instrumental music" and passed a motion by a vote of twenty-three to one stating that "we [First Baptist] are in favor of instrumental music."[32] Though the minutes do not reveal the role that Carroll played in this discussion, the size of the vote indicates that the motion had his strong support.

Carroll eventually did make his opinion on church music known in a series of articles which appeared in the *Texas Baptist Herald*. In these articles he debated the opinions of Adam Clark, who was deceased. At the conclusion of the first article, Carroll stated his reasons for writing the articles and for debating a dead man:

> I have a serious reason for writing on this subject, and a facetious reason for making a dead man my opponent. The serious reason is that the subject of church music is worthy of thought, prayer, investigation and criticism. The facetious reason is that a dead man cannot provoke me into a newspaper controversy, which I greatly deprecate. As I do not propose to take any advantage of him, I suppose it will make no difference with the illustrious dead.[33]

In one article Carroll stated his belief that the sole purpose of the church choir was to lead and to unify the congregational singing; for the choir to sing by itself "is worse than an absurdity. It is a sin when habitual."[34] As with all articles that Carroll wrote to defend or to explain a position, his arguments concerning church music were heavily supported by scripture.

Another of Carroll's innovative ideas was the use of women in the deacon ministry of the church, a fact which oddly enough receives only a brief mention in Burkhalter's history of First Baptist. The church appointed six women to serve as deaconesses in April 1877, with their primary duties listed as "assisting the deacons in ministering to the poor of the congregation and helping in the baptism of the women and girl candidates."[35] These appointments represent the only time during Carroll's pastorate, as well as in the history of the church, where records state that women were appointed to the deacon ministry.

In reflecting upon the office of deaconesses some years later, Carroll wrote:

In my own experience as pastor and especially in administration of what is called the poor fund of the church, we often found, where the applicant for aid was a woman, that discreet women members of the church could find out better the propriety of aiding the case in question than men could do.[36]

In the same article, however, he carefully noted that:

There is not anything in the Scriptures to indicate that deaconesses should be ordained. There is no teaching on that subject. They simply received appointment from the church. As a pastor I found great help from a number of deaconesses that at my suggestion were appointed by the church.[37]

REVIVAL/FIRE

In January 1876, the church voted to extend the sanctuary and to install a baptistry. In retrospect these actions seem almost prophetic, for both the sanctuary extension and the baptistry were in use during the spring of 1876. The revival that took place at First Baptist that spring is called by Burkhalter "the most outstanding event of the first ten years of Carroll's pastorate."[38] Ironically, however, Carroll had little to do with the revival. Conducted by W. E. Penn, the revival began in April and lasted a total of eighty-one days. Each time that it drew to a close, the church voted to continue the meetings.[39] The *Texas Baptist Herald* reported that as a result of the revival:

There have been about 370 conversions. There have been 152 baptized, five await baptism, eight have been restored, 34 received by letter, and seven are under watch care until letters are secured.[40]

Even though Carroll played only a small part in the revival, he had now assumed the responsibility for a much larger congregation than he had previously led. Unfortunately, Carroll was not physically able to perform his duties. The minutes of Sunday, July 20, 1876, record:

Our pastor, though in feeble health, preached for us today at 11 o'clock a.m. He spoke in demonstration of the Spirit and with great power and effect. We were all somewhat sad that we are to be separated from him for one month for physical recuperation in the month of August.[41]

The month of recuperation apparently allowed Carroll to regain his health and to return to his duties in September.

In a move that doubtlessly surprised the church, Carroll tendered his resignation as pastor a short time later, on February 18, 1877. After much discussion the church accepted his resignation and immediately reelected Carroll as pastor, although he did not immediately accept. The events that led to his resignation are unknown; and Burkhalter's detailed history of the church makes no mention of it. Carroll may have resigned because the church was behind on his salary, for a motion occurs in the minutes to pay the balance due the pastor by the following month. But Carroll may also have resigned for another reason — First Baptist, San Antonio, had extended a call to him several months earlier.[42]

This resignation was not the first indication of trouble between First Baptist and its pastor.[43]

Carroll's resignation was soon overshadowed by the greatest tragedy in the history of the church. On February 22, 1877, a fire that had originated in the City Market Opera House adjacent to First Baptist destroyed the church building. Meeting in the Church of Christ sanctuary on February 25, church members mourned the loss of their building. Yet they also saw the loss as a blessing. In a preamble and resolutions drafted at this meeting, church members admitted that their former building had limitations; and they outlined the type of building that they planned to construct.[44] The congregation held its services in the chapel of Waco University until 1880, when builders had partially completed the new sanctuary and services could be held there. The entire building was finally completed in 1883.

At the February 25 meeting in 1877, Carroll announced that he would continue to serve as pastor. He stated that he had resigned in "good faith," but "since that time he finds that he had misunderstood some things of which now being correctly advised his mind is changed."[45] This incident is the first of three recorded times that Carroll considered leaving First Baptist. On each occasion the church resolved a problem that allowed Carroll to stay. In many ways Carroll appears to have manipulated First Baptist to do his will by threatening to leave.[46]

THE RISING STAR AMONG SOUTHERN BAPTISTS

No past historian has mentioned Carroll's personal contact with alcohol in discussing Carroll's role in the Prohibition Movement. The family's custom of drinking whiskey every morning had a direct effect on Carroll's later role in the movement.

Carroll began to support an active ban on the possession and consumption of alcohol sometime prior to 1873. On December 14 of that year, Carroll, along with a committee of five, recommended that the church adopt five resolutions dealing with temperance. The fourth, and most controversial of the resolutions, stated:

> Resolved, fourth, That under the force and guidance of these great principles of love, charity, and forbearance, we do hereby solemnly agree among ourselves not to drink at all of any intoxicating liquors, brandy, wine, whiskey, ale, porter, lager beer, cider, and the like, in any of their forms, and that we will not be ourselves the judge as to when it shall be administered medicinally, but that even as a medicine, we will only receive it in case of absolute necessity upon the prescription of an honest, fair, truth-loving physician.[47]

Discussions on the resolutions lasted six hours, ending near midnight. During the evening some church members presented a substitute motion that simply stated: "Resolved, that as a church we covenant to abstain from the use of or traffic in intoxicating liquor as a beverage."[48] This motion was defeated. Finally, the original motion was approved sixty to fourteen. Carroll noted later that the church supported temperance seventy-four to zero, a number which included the fourteen dissenters who were not opposed to temperance but had voted for the substitute motion instead.

Because of the growing interest in temperance among Baptists, J. B. Link asked Carroll to give a full report on the actions of First Baptist in the *Texas Baptist Herald*. In the January 8, 1874, issue, Carroll reviewed the actions of the church and expressed his pride at the stand that First Baptist had taken. Exhibiting a rather candid view of how divisive the temperance issue was among Baptists at this time, he stated:

> We may not have taken exactly the right stand; we are fallible; we know and cheerfully concede it. That we are in harmony with the principles of Christianity, we humbly believe. Time, experience, and resignation may soften down some asperities, may suggest some changes.[49]

Though Carroll seemed to imply that there was room for a "softer" stand on temperance, he never wavered from the hard line taken in the original resolutions of First Baptist. Little information exists on any further role that Carroll had in the Prohibition Movement during his early ministry. One document that has survived is a letter to Carroll from an official with the Democratic Party in Texas in 1878. The tone of the letter indicated that by 1878, many saw Carroll as a leader in the growing Prohibition Movement. In the letter the official pleaded with Carroll to stop emphasizing temperance for the good of the party. The official believed that the time to address prohibition politically had not yet come. Carroll apparently heeded his advice. He did not become active again politically with the Prohibition Democrats on the issue of temperance until well into the 1880s.[50]

Carroll's stand on the issue of temperance during the early part of his ministry was a progressive one. He helped to standardize the attitudes of many Baptists on prohibition in the early stages of the movement. As a member of this early vanguard for the fight against alcohol, Carroll naturally would become one of the major leaders of the movement as the prohibition issue matured in the 1880s.

WACO UNIVERSITY

Carroll's first contact with Waco University came in June 1866, when, at the age of twenty-two, he addressed the students at the commencement exercises.[51] After becoming pastor of First Baptist in 1870, he addressed the student body on numerous occasions. From the moment that he arrived in Waco, Carroll was a strong supporter of Waco University. Burleson, his old friend and president of the school, no doubt encouraged his involvement.

In 1873 Carroll initiated a program for training ministerial students at the university, and according to Jeff D. Ray this training had evolved by 1880 into an "embryonic theological seminary." This "class," consisting of fifteen young ministers, was held on Friday nights in Carroll's home.[52]

Carroll's support of the school was not limited to his involvement with the students. In 1873 Waco University named Carroll as a trustee. In this role Carroll was part of the first attempt to consolidate Baylor and Waco University in 1875. Though the extent of Carroll's involvement in the meeting is unknown, Carroll's brother J. M. notes that Carroll kept the crowd awake with his "wholesome humor."

The meeting also created the Central Baptist Educational Commission and directed the new agency to raise money to create a central Baptist school. Carroll was nominated twice to become the fundraising agent for the commission, but he declined both times. The commission experienced great initial success but eventually failed. The outcome might have been different had Carroll, who was now becoming a prominent spokesman for Christian education, accepted the fundraising post. In 1877, however, Carroll stated that he had reservations concerning the commission from its inception and had only voted for it because "great" men had supported the plan.[53]

DENOMINATIONAL WORK

Carroll's denominational work during his early ministry took place at two levels — associational and state. At both levels Burleson apparently served as his personal "letter of introduction." The *Waco Association Minutes* first mention Carroll's name in 1870. The following year the association named him to a special committee dealing with education.[54] By 1874 Carroll had firmly established himself as a leader; and the association named him president of the mission board, a position that he would hold until 1888. As president his duties were:

> to visit during the year every church in Waco Association, and hold mass meetings in the mission interest, and instruct the churches and impress missionary duty. That this visit be appointed after consultation with pastor of each church, and the meeting held under the sanction of the church.[55]

Through this position Carroll had a great influence on all the churches within the association.

Carroll's involvement at the state level began in 1871, when he presented a report on "Schools and Education" to the Baptist General Association of Texas. In this report Carroll challenged the General Association to begin a campaign to raise $30,000 for Waco University. No doubt many of the people in attendance wondered how this young man, relatively new to the General Association, could make such a challenge. This fundraising campaign was possibly Burleson's idea, with Carroll serving only as the presenter.[56]

From the beginning of Carroll's involvement with the General Association, fellow Baptists apparently recognized his leadership ability. With Burleson's support and the notoriety that Carroll had gained from his debate with Fisher, by 1874 Carroll had established himself as an important figure in the General Association just as he had done with the Waco Association. From 1871 to 1885 the asso-

ciation elected Carroll as vice-president of the general body while
Burleson served as its president. During this time Carroll helped the
General Association to work more effectively than it previously had
worked by aiding in its restructuring and initiating constitutional
changes. One of Carroll's more innovative suggestions came in
1878. After presenting a report on missions which cited the confusion caused by the numerous missions offerings collected during the
year, Carroll suggested that one "great mission" offering be taken,
and then be properly divided by the churches. This suggestion re-
sembles a primitive Cooperative Program approach at the local
level.[57] Carroll's leadership also played a role in the founding of
Buckner Orphans' Home in 1877 and in the messenger controversy
involving First Baptist, Dallas, in 1880.[58]

EARLY CONTROVERSIES

Carroll, as documented, never ran away from a good fight. As a
result he found himself in the middle of numerous denominational
controversies during his lifetime, with the first two occurring in
these early years of ministry.

The Carroll-Compere Controversy, as J. W. Crowder designates
it, might better be termed a debate. In 1875 Thomas H. Compere responded to a controversial statement that Carroll had made before the
Waco Association in August 1874. There Carroll stated:

> Any man who, faithfully consecrating himself, trusting alone in
> God, and presenting the duty of the churches, yet comes to
> paupery, proves by his starvation that he was not called of God.[59]

Compere, corresponding secretary for the Richland Association, attempted to show the fallacy of Carroll's argument through
the example of W. H. Parks, a missionary serving the Richland Association. Compere noted that Parks was an effective minister, yet
the Richland Association was having trouble raising money to support his family and him. Carroll responded in the *Texas Baptist Herald* on February 4, 1875, by asking Compere to give examples of
men who were called of God and yet had starved.

The debate continued for six months in the pages of the *Herald*. Carroll's basic argument was that true Christian ministers
called of God would receive the financial support necessary to sur-
vive as full-time ministers and should by faith believe that they
would not starve. In examining this argument Compere questioned:

Why is it that the Lord always calls and sends those who are supported by faith to those places where the money is ready, not to be raised by faith but paid over by contract.[60]

As in many newspaper debates there was no clear winner when the controversy disappeared from the pages of the *Herald* in the latter half of 1875. Carroll's stand on the issue is somewhat surprising, given his early financial struggles as a young minister in and around Caldwell. The debate might have been different had Compere been aware of Carroll's early struggles. Believing that he should be a full-time minister, Carroll had to leave Post Oak, where he could not support himself, to become the pastor of New Hope, where the salary was higher. Though Carroll never stated the matter directly in his arguments with Compere, he alluded to a belief that all ministers called of God should be able to work full-time on the field.[61]

The creation of the East Texas Baptist Convention in 1877 was the second controversy in which Carroll was involved during his early ministry. On December 12, 1877, eighteen churches met at Overton to form the convention. In his December 20 editorial in the *Herald*, J. B. Link gave a favorable report of the organizational meeting.[62] In response, on January 17, 1878, Carroll presented eight arguments against the forming of the new convention. Baptists were currently discussing the consolidation of the General Association and the State Convention; a third body would only complicate the process.[63] Link, however, saw the new convention as a symbol of the displeasure of East Texas Baptists with the General Association.

The articles on the East Texas Baptist Convention revealed the mutual distrust of Carroll and Link; each accused the other of hidden agendas in their discussions of Baptist work in Texas. As the controversy continued, the issue of the new convention faded to be replaced by the issue of which man best understood the hearts and minds of Texas Baptists. Here again there was no clear winner; both Carroll and Link could point to their supporters. Perhaps the only real outcome of this controversy was to delay further the consolidation of the state bodies.[64]

Keith Cogburn believes that Carroll's actions in this controversy damaged his own reputation rather than Link's as Carroll had intended. Cogburn states: "By the late 1870s many Baptists perceived the young champion of orthodoxy as arrogant and vindictive."[65] Some Baptists did perceive Carroll this way; however, many of these people were against him from the beginning of the controversy with Link. Carroll's reputation remained undamaged for those who supported him. This controversy would not be the last time that those who disagreed with Carroll saw him as "arrogant or vindictive."

THE SOUTHERN BAPTIST CONVENTION

Unlike his position at the state and associational levels, Carroll's role in the Southern Baptist Convention was not a prominent one during his early ministry. The *Southern Baptist Convention Minutes* first mention Carroll's name in 1874, when the convention appointed him to a committee dealing with "the enlargement of Home Missions." In 1878 Carroll received the highest honor of his young ministry when Southern Baptists selected him to bring the convention sermon.

Carroll delivered the sermon, entitled "The Providence of God and the Christian Life," with such power that he was appointed to preach at every future convention that he attended.[66] Carroll's first appearance in the Southern Baptist Convention spotlight, however, instigated a response which Carroll abhorred throughout his ministry—criticism. In the *Baptist Reflector*, Tennessee's state paper, an anonymous writer questioned Carroll's contention that ordination was essential to the office of preacher. In his response to this criticism Carroll alluded to the cowardly nature of the writer for not signing his name. He then addressed, but never refuted, the arguments raised by the writer.[67] This aversion to accept criticism or to be questioned was a major weakness in Carroll. He performed each aspect of his ministry with the confidence that he was within the will of God; therefore, his opinions and interpretations were always correct.

THE PRICE OF FAME

Upon Carroll's return from the Southern Baptist Convention in 1878, rumors began to circulate concerning his divorce. The reason that this issue surfaced after so many years is unclear. During this same time a major controversy was growing between the two state denominational papers — the *Texas Baptist Herald*, operated by J. B. Link, and the *Texas Baptist*, operated by R. C. Buckner and for whom Carroll was an editor. M. V. Smith believed that Carroll's role in the newspaper controversy as well as his growing popularity,

FBC, Waco building completed in 1883.
— Courtesy Southwestern Baptist Theological Seminary Archives

both in and out of Texas, caused Carroll's "great tragedy" to be brought to light.[68]

By the summer of 1878 the rumors had reached a point where they had to be stopped. Smith, who was pastor of First Baptist, Belton, investigated the situation and found evidence which clearly showed that Carroll's first wife had committed adultery and then left him. This fact removed Carroll's responsibility for the divorce. Smith then presented his information to First Baptist, Waco. Whether his report informed the church of the divorce itself or simply put the details into written form is unclear from the church minutes. The church took no action concerning the report. With Carroll's permission the *Texas Baptist Herald* printed the report by Smith later that summer. Perhaps in an effort to convince his readers that he had nothing to do with Carroll's divorce coming to light,[69] Link clearly states in an explanation preceding the article that he was publishing the report with Carroll's knowledge.

OPEN HOUSE AT WACO

In 1882, as builders applied the finishing touches to the new First Baptist sanctuary, Carroll invited the Southern Baptist Convention to hold its annual meeting at the church. The convention declined for 1882 but accepted for 1883. The 1883 convention was the first to which women were invited to attend and, as a result, it drew a large crowd. In recording the historic event, J. W. Jenkins writes:

> On the 9th instant, the Southern Baptist Convention, according to agreement, met with our church. We had expected originally 1,000 delegates and visitors, which was nearly 400 more than any other church had ever entertained. And we were somewhat doubtful of our ability to entertain this number when it became certain there would be that many. And when the ever-increasing list went up to 1,500 we were alarmed and began at once to notify our Texas brethren that we could not entertain them. But when that list had grown to 2,500 we were appalled.[70]

First Baptist accommodated all who came, though the facilities were cramped at times. Ray states that Carroll had over thirty ministers in his home alone.

SUMMARY

The Southern Baptist Convention of 1883 signaled the end of an era for B. H. Carroll and First Baptist, Waco, though the best years for both lay ahead. In Carroll's first thirteen years as pastor of First Baptist, membership grew from 201 to 426. Carroll led the church in trying innovative ideas in music and in ministry. He helped to guide the church through its first major crisis in the loss of its building. And most importantly, as a result of his attempted resignations, Carroll came to realize that the church needed him more than he needed the church. While at First Baptist, Carroll also became an active leader in denominational affairs at the associational, state, and convention levels.

What can one conclude from this review of Carroll's early ministry, and what role did this early ministry play in his later life? The answer to these questions is simple. Carroll's early ministry was foundational to his achievements for the rest of his life. The Fisher debate prepared him for M. T. Martin. Training ministers in his home prepared him for the founding of Southwestern Seminary. Carroll's early stand for temperance led to his becoming a leader in the Prohibition Movement. And his early mission endeavors laid the groundwork for his address on Home Missions to the Southern Baptist Convention in 1888. Carroll's early ministry, especially his pastorate at First Baptist, Waco, was a time in which he built his stage — a stage that he would play upon for the rest of his life.

CHAPTER 3

The Maturing Leader

THE RENOWNED PREACHER

By the time Carroll's ministry at First Baptist Church, Waco, had reached the halfway mark, he not only had become well known for his preaching skill and leadership ability at the local and state levels but at the national level as well. Churches from around the Southern Baptist Convention offered him their pulpits, yet he chose to remain in Waco. By the 1890s Carroll had risen to such stature within the Southern Baptist Convention that John R. Sampey, professor at Southern Seminary, wrote to him:

> I will say to your face what I have many times said behind your back, that you now — since Broadus is gone — are our natural leader in the Southern Convention.[1]

Carroll's skill as a communicator was the tool which allowed him, a frontier pastor on the outer boundary of the convention, to rise to such prominence.

CARROLL'S CONCEPT OF PREACHING

In "A Sermon to Preachers," a message delivered before the Baptist General Convention of Texas in 1892, Carroll explained the power of preaching and the awesome responsibility that he felt accompanied the task:

I never stand up to preach without trembling. It is not stage fright, for perhaps I esteem too slightly the judgment of men or women whether expressed in praise or censure. But there is something about preaching which affects me even more than the approach of death. I never refuse to preach on any proper occasion, when invited — I love to preach. I was not driven into the ministry. I never fled from God's message like Jonah. I never hide behind modest apologies, but I never in life stood up to preach except once (which exception I profoundly regret) without first isolating myself from all human company, even the dearest, and prostrating myself in spirit before the dread and awful God, imploring him, in deepest humility, to bless me that one time. Perhaps I am wrong. I would not judge harshly, but I cannot rid myself of the conviction that the man who can lightly — who can arrogantly — who can with brazen effrontery of manner — get up in the pulpit — get up unstaggered with the weight of responsibility resting on him — get up as an ambassador for God as if God were his ambassador — is disqualified for this holy office.[2]

He continued, stating that if a man does not realize the importance of preaching then he should not preach, regardless of how well he speaks, how much he knows, or how many admirers he has. He was highly critical of those who felt that preaching was a skill that could be practiced:

Did you ever, in your life, hear of a preacher noted for habitually reaching souls, for leading thousands to Christ, who stood before a mirror and studied the postures and gesticulation with which to ornament his sermon?[3]

Though Carroll believed that a preacher was a messenger, not an actor, he did not dismiss the importance of delivery in effectively communicating a message. He believed that good delivery came as a result of prayerful preparation; and if a preacher would carefully seek the spirit of God, the "manner and gesticulation" would "take care of itself."[4]

While a preacher should depend upon God in sermon preparation, Carroll felt that a preacher should depend upon himself in biblical study. If a man's study was lackadaisical, he would be unable to preach effectively. As an illustration of this point he highlighted the life of a young preacher who was a brilliant speaker yet never studied. Carroll met with the young man and told him that unless he studied the Word his sermons would become redundant and lose their power of persuasion. The young man disregarded Carroll's advice. Carroll noted that as a result, "he [the young man] never stays longer than two years with any one church, because in that time he tells all he knows and some he doesn't know."[5]

For Carroll the call to preach came from God, and preaching itself was a divine act:

> When I want to impress a thought, I first ask, ought it be done? Then I get before Him with whom is power and ask Him to give me power.[6]

According to Carroll the most effective preachers were those who continually studied scripture and sought the spirit of God. Clear communication skills and a good delivery would be a natural by-product of God's working through the preacher.

Carroll may have de-emphasized the importance of sermon delivery because it was never a problem for him. He probably would not have risen to prominence in the Southern Baptist Convention, however, had he not been able to draw upon his experience as a speaker and a debater and instead had been forced to rely on his "manner and gesticulation" to "take care of itself."

HIS PRESENCE

When Carroll's contemporaries described him as a preacher, they began with a physical description. At six feet four inches tall and weighing over 260 pounds, Carroll was a giant among the men of his day, not only behind the pulpit but in the boardroom as well. C. B. Williams believes that Carroll's physique gave him "a fifteen to twenty percent advantage over a preacher or speaker with a lean and unattractive body."[7] Although Williams' numbers are figuratively based, considering Carroll's size and speaking ability, fundamental accuracy of this claim is difficult to dispute.

With his long, flowing, white beard, Carroll reminded Jeff D. Ray of a prophet. His gray eyes, which were usually "mild and benevolent," could be piercing during an argument or burn like fire during a speech or sermon.[8]

S. P. Brooks believes that Carroll's giant physique actually attracted some to hear him preach.[9] And Williams implies that Carroll's physical presence intimidated his audience into listening to him:

> His imposing figure put the audience in a receptive mood and

helped sustain the interest as he rose to climaxes of ponderous thinking and to periods of eloquent expression.[10]

Carroll was well aware of his physical advantage over most men of his day; and he would use this advantage often when he was speaking, debating, preaching, or merely observing.

HIS INTELLECT

Although Carroll was unable to complete his formal education, he had a great capacity for learning. He developed a unique reading style which allowed him to read and comprehend two to four lines on a page at once.[11] His ability to read and digest books became almost legendary. Reportedly for the vast majority of his life, he read an average of 300 pages a day, making careful notes in the margins citing reasons that he agreed or disagreed with the author.[12]

Carroll's memory was not photographic, but he possessed an uncanny ability to remember what he had read. In his later years Carroll's brother J. M. recalls one particular incident:

On one occasion I went to Waco to see him. Without knocking, I walked into his study. He was writing an article for some paper. He raised his head, saw who I was (I had not seen him for months) and simply remarked, "Hello, Jimmie *[sic]*; wait awhile; I will talk with you directly; I am nearly through this article." He did not stop to even shake hands with me, but continued his writing, and in a moment he raised his head and said to me, "Jimmy, you can help me a little and I will get through quicker. I want a book. It is in a certain room" (which he designated as there were books in all the halls, and in every room on the place). He continued his writing, but told me how to find and recognize the book. It was in a certain case on the third shelf from the top about sixteen inches from the left-hand end of the shelf. I found the book instantly, just where he said, and carried it to him. He did not lift his head. He kept writing and simply said, "You can find what I want" (I had never read the book); "I want only to refresh my memory of a story." He hesitated for one brief moment from his writing, and then said, "Look — on page — about 143 — about one-third of the way down the page and you will find the story." I looked and it was there. I then asked him, "How long since you read this book?" He answered, "At least fifteen years." "Have you looked in it since?" "Not once."[13]

Carroll's memory provided him with an invaluable resource

from which he often drew when addressing an audience. In his "un-biased" appraisal Williams believes that Carroll's intellect "approxi-mated, and in some sense possibly surpassed, Aristotle and [Fran-cis] Bacon."[14]

HIS MESSAGE

The majority of Carroll's sermons were expository; however, he also addressed some topical issues such as baptism, the Lord's Supper, and the church.[15] Carroll had excellent control of the En-glish language and communicated clearly, although his messages were not necessarily easy to understand. Often his sermons on doc-trinal issues became tedious and technical, making it difficult for the congregation to follow his message.[16] Although they might not have understood Carroll's arguments, the audience was usually persuad-ed to endorse his conclusion by the power of his delivery.

Although some of Carroll's sermons were technical and diffi-cult to understand, the majority were straightforward. Carroll often used his debate background to call upon the congregation to make a decision. In his sermon "The Agnostic," delivered with the forceful style for which Carroll became known, he stated:

> Try a benevolent philosophy. It lifts a lordly head. It shakes a kingly crest. It attitudinizes as a mighty one. And what is it? Ag-nosticism! What is agnosticism? It is a philosophy of not-know-ing. Is there any final healing? It answers, "I don't know." If my heart is burdened, is there any hope in kneeling down and praying "God, Help me?" It croaks, "I don't know." And a man prides himself on that, and goes around pushing common peoples aside, and says, "Here is a philosophy for you." What? "The philosophy of not knowing anything." How will that heal the world? How will that stay the hand of the assassin? How will that reform? How will it redeem the bondman? How will it strike the shackles from the slave? How will it shove off Satan, whose cloven foot presses down on the heart of the fallen? It can have no power. It is a negation, just a negation.
>
> What will you put in place of the gospel? Here are the con-duits that convey this water of life to the world. Shall we break them up? Here is the aqueduct. Shall we cut it down? Tear down the churches? Fold up the banner and close the book? Let men quit praying? The fool hath said in his heart, "No God! No God!"[17]

CONTINUED WORK WITH PROHIBITION

In 1878 Carroll ceased his active work with the temperance movement following a plea by an official with the Democratic Party who promised that the Democrats would address the issue in the future. The United Friends of Temperance held a meeting in Waco in July 1885. At this time the state constitution provided for local option elections on prohibition. The United Friends of Temperance, however, passed a resolution at their meeting calling for an amendment to the state constitution enforcing prohibition. In an effort to gauge their strength, the group proposed that a referendum be held for McLennan County on August 31, 1885.

They asked Carroll, who was not a member of the group, to lead the prohibition force during the campaign. Carroll believed that the time had come once again for him to address temperance. Frustrated with the Democratic Party's insensitivity to the prohibitionists, he agreed to lead the force, opening the campaign in early August.

For Carroll, prohibition was a moral rather than a political fight. He asserted the right of a community to protect itself from dangerous influences, and he dismissed the assertations by anti-prohibitionists that passage of the referendum would doom the future of Waco.[18]

The campaign was not a political fight for the anti-prohibitionists either but a battle to preserve personal liberties and the Democratic Party.[19] To oppose Carroll, they called upon two well-known politicians — Senator Richard Coke and Congressman Roger Q. Mills. The *Waco Examiner*, owned by an anti-prohibitionist, became their mouthpiece. Mills saw prohibition as an "invasion of the right of personal self government." He believed that an infringement on personal liberty would also endanger civil, political, and religious liberties.[20]

Carroll addressed anti-prohibitionist concerns in an article which appeared in the *Galveston Daily News* on August 12, 1885. Admitting that it was unusual for a preacher to be as active as he in an election, Carroll noted once again that prohibition was a moral rather than a political issue. He also admitted that if prohibition did pass, some personal liberties would have to be surrendered for the good of the community. Carroll discounted the charge that prohibitionists were attempting to damage the Democratic Party by pointing out that it was the Democrats who had put the local option clause in the constitution. The prohibitionists were only attempting to exercise an option given to them by the Democratic Party. Carroll also dismissed the claim that prohibition would damage the local economy by asserting that the cotton industry, the heart of the economy, would be unaffected by prohibition.[21]

The article appearing in the *Daily News* was produced from a sermon delivered by Carroll. Soon after its appearance Carroll began to receive requests for the sermon from all over the state. Prohibitionists in other Texas cities began to write to Carroll asking for advice on conducting their own campaigns.[22] As the election approached, Carroll clearly emerged as the leader of prohibition forces in Texas, making him an easy target for the anti-prohibitionists.

During the campaign, Carroll often preached on prohibition. Some accused him of using his pulpit for stump speeches; others called him a "would be politician" who had no understanding of political matters.[23] Surprisingly, considering Carroll's history as a fighter, he never responded to the personal attacks thrown at him throughout his involvement with the Prohibition Movement. Perhaps he realized that responding to the attacks or going on the offensive would shift the campaign from one of issues to one of personalities. By refusing to counterattack, Carroll was able to keep the movement focused during the final days preceding the election.

The climactic event of the campaign took place on Saturday, August 29, two days before the election. The anti-prohibitionists had arranged a barbecue at which Coke and Mills would speak. In noting the large attendance, the *Waco Day* stated that many had come to hear Coke attack Carroll.[24]

During the rally both Coke and Mills focused their attention not on the pending election but on personal attacks against Carroll. Coke warned other preachers that following Carroll's example could endanger the separation of church and state. He accused Carroll of hiding behind his pulpit in an effort to avoid direct debate with the opposition. During this speech Coke issued his famous statement directed toward Carroll and the ministers who followed him. Coke shouted: "If your parsons go into politics, scourge them back by stopping their rations."[25]

In February 1886, Coke wrote to Carroll and apologized for the remarks that he made during this speech, but at the same time he defended his position:

> I do not hesitate to say that while last fall when under the high
> excitement of the canvas I did refer to you in terms which I have

since much regretted, that this feeling has passed away with the occassion [sic] which produced it, and that I feel toward you the same respect and esteem and even more than regard that I have always felt for you, and as all my friends know I have been constantly in the habit of expressing for you for years. You may be right in your views on Prohibition. I do not think you are. I believe you are in error, as you think I am. We are both honest in our opinions and have a right to entertain them. You do not believe it a political question. I entertain no doubt but that it fills every definition of a political question. Here again we honestly differ. You believe it right to take this question into the church and discuss it from the pulpit. I believe it radically wrong to do so, that it is hurtful to both church and religion to do it. I do not question the honesty of your convictions as I know you do not mine. No man has ever regretted more than myself that I am naturally and incurably rough in my mode of expression on the stump. My convictions are very earnest and my expressions of them partake of the same character. I say this as a predicate for the assurance that I sincerely regret ever having made any remark in that canvass which could in the slightest degree grate upon our feelings, and further, that no vestige or shadow of that which prompted any such remark, remains to cloud or mar my old time esteem confidence in and sincere regard for you. It is said that 'an honest confession is good for the soul', [sic] and I feel better for having made a statement to you, which simply does myself justice, while meeting in a proper and becoming manner the kindly spirit of your letter.[26]

Stunned by news of the rally, Carroll responded the next morning by stating that his role in the campaign was that of a "watchman" to "sound the trumpet and warn the people." In addressing the personal attacks made upon him, he declared:

I knew that it would make me a target for the archers. I knew that it would subject me to foul aspersion and misrepresentation. I knew that there was for me neither money nor glory in it.[27]

After stating that he held no ill feelings toward Coke, Mills, and others who had attacked him, Carroll closed by saying:

As for myself, I can do no other than stand where I do. As a friend of humanity, a Christian, and a Democrat, I must vote for prohibition.[28]

Amidst fear of a split within the Democratic Party and concern for personal liberty, the referendum for prohibition in McLennan

County failed by nearly a three-to-one margin. *The Houston Age* wrote: "Brother Carroll . . . will probably decide that he had better stick to the pulpit and fight the devil."[29] Papers around the state saw the defeat as the death knell for the Prohibition Movement. But Carroll remained unbowed and resolved never to be silent on prohibition again.

Disappointed by the McLennan County defeat and the outcome of the Democratic State Convention of 1868, the extreme prohibitionists split from the Democrats to form their own party. J. B. Cranfill, publisher of the *Waco Advance* and member of First Baptist Church, led the new party. Although the prohibitionist candidate for governor received only six percent of the vote in 1886, Democrats feared that the new party could be a sufficient political force in the future if the legislature did not address the prohibition question. In an effort to ease political tension and bring the extreme prohibitionists back into the Democratic Party, a prohibition amendment was placed on the ballot for an August 4, 1887, vote.[30]

While Cranfill pursued a political route to bring about prohibition, Carroll became active in a non-political organization, the State Prohibition Alliance, whose goal was statewide prohibition. The founding of the Texas Prohibition Party in 1886 had divided prohibitionists into two camps — those who saw prohibition as a political issue and those who did not. In an effort to bring the two sides together, Cranfill called for a meeting of all prohibitionists in Waco in March 1887. At this meeting the prohibitionists united into one group, the Non-Partisan Prohibition Amendment Organization; and a state central committee was formed to head the amendment fight. Members selected Carroll to chair the committee and Waco to become the headquarters.[31]

First Baptist, Waco, granted Carroll a three-month leave so that he could dedicate himself to the campaign. With this freedom he traveled throughout the state, speaking and writing articles for Cranfill's paper. Using his debate background he answered the concerns of the anti-prohibitionists by providing evidence that a positive rather than negative impact had been felt in communities where prohibition had passed. He cited Atlanta, Kansas, and Maine as examples where prohibition had brought about improved social conditions and a reduction in taxes.[32] Carroll often quoted Thomas Jefferson and James Madison, two creators of personal liberty, in his speeches and articles to show that the personal liberty argument used so effectively by anti-prohibitionists in the Waco campaign had been misrepresented.[33]

Prohibition was a nonpolitical issue for Carroll, but his close association with the politically active Cranfill led many to believe that Carroll had political ambitions of his own. Some felt that if prohibition passed, Carroll would be nominated by the Texas Prohibition Party for the United States Senate.[34] Carroll's personal papers, however, reveal no evidence of political ambitions. Such speculation threatened to split the fragile alliance between the political and nonpolitical prohibitionists. In an effort to keep the campaign away from the political arena, Carroll began to distance himself from Cranfill and the *Waco Advance*.

In July 1887, Carroll debated one of his chief opponents, Roger Q. Mills, face to face, a method which had not been used in the Mc-Lennan County campaign. Perhaps Carroll debated Mills because of earlier criticism that he was hiding behind his pulpit, or perhaps face to face confrontation was simply a change in his strategy. During this campaign Carroll, likewise, did not refrain from a personal attack on Mills as he had in the McLennan County campaign. In fact, the two men spent three hours exchanging insults and accusations rather than focusing on the issue of prohibition. At one point Carroll taunted Mills with poetry:

> Ah, Roger the Dodger!
> Thou mayest dodge good and
> Thou mayest dodge evil, but
> With all thy dodging, thou
> Canst not dodge the devil![35]

Mills responded by pointing his finger at Carroll and shouting: "Hell is full of better than that man, so full that their legs hang out the windows." As the debate came to a close, Mills produced a note allegedly written by Carroll while living with his family in Caldwell. The note, addressed to a local grocer, read: "Please charge my whiskey account to my father as fruit, candy, etc." Carroll immediately rose and asked Mills to withdraw the note, claiming that it was a forgery. With crowd control dissipating rapidly, Mills complied, stating: "Mr. Carroll did not write it."[36] The debate succeeded in stirring the crowd, but failed in changing votes.[37]

Like Coke before him, Mills eventually apologized to Carroll in a letter dated May 1, 1896:

In the heated prohibition campaign, in a moment of political excitement and political bitterness among our people, you and I had an unfortunate formal debate, in which I used language toward you of which I have been ashamed ever since. Before that, then, and ever since, I have regarded you as a pure sincere, Christian gentleman and before I go hence and be no more I wanted to say to you that I regretted that language and now sincerely apologize to you for its use. I hope you may have many years yet to serve your church and your country, and no friend of yours will rejoice more sincerely at your prosperity and happiness than I.[38]

The prohibition amendment had failed once again by an almost two-to-one margin. H. William Schneider believed that nonpolitical prohibitionists loyal to the Democratic Party refused to vote for the amendment for fear that it would strengthen the Texas Prohibition Party, making it a political force. This fear, in effect, defeated the amendment.

After the campaign, Carroll returned to his work at First Baptist; however, many now saw him as a political force and ally. In an effort to heal the Democratic Party, N. W. Finley, the state chairman, wrote to Carroll asking him to campaign for the Democratic ticket in 1888. Carroll declined, but in an open letter to Finley he did endorse the Democratic ticket with the exception of Mills. In declining the opportunity to campaign, Carroll sent a clear message that ministers should not engage in political activity. In reference to his work for prohibition, Carroll repeatedly described his role as nonpartisan.

Through both campaigns Carroll remained true to his convictions that prohibition was a moral rather than a political issue. Morally, Carroll was a prohibitionist who would continue to support the movement; politically he was a Democrat.

Although Carroll emerged from the Prohibition Movement of the 1880s as a defender of morality, the grocer's note produced by Mills left a dent in this knight's armor. The note was dismissed by Carroll as a forgery; but according to the autobiography of J. M., such a note could have been written during Carroll's early days in Caldwell. J. M. states openly that whiskey nearly destroyed some of the Carroll family with B. H., himself, nearly becoming part of a "harvest of hard drinkers." These family experiences could have provided Carroll with a powerful personal testimony on the dangers of whiskey, yet at no time does he ever mention his contact with alcohol. An outsider judging Carroll's reaction to the grocer's note would have found any connection between Carroll and whiskey impossible to believe. The reluctance to disclose his experience with alcohol reinforces Carroll's difficulty in admitting weakness. By hiding such weaknesses, Carroll became a superhuman figure in the eyes of many Baptists.[39]

DENOMINATIONAL LEADERSHIP

Although Carroll's prominence at both the state and national levels increased, he continued to remain active in local Baptist affairs. At the 1888 associational meeting, Carroll tendered his resignation as chairman of the Mission Board, a position that he had held for fourteen years. He stated no reason for resigning; however, he may have been exhausted from his other responsibilities. This same year Carroll was named as the Waco Baptist Association's first messenger to the Southern Baptist Convention.[40]

The greatest impact that Carroll had in the Waco Baptist Association occurred in the early 1890s, during the M. T. Martin Controversy (to be discussed later). When the association needed stable leadership of the Mission Board during this time, Carroll reconsidered his resignation and accepted the appointment to serve as chairman. Without his leadership during the controversy, the association might not have survived.

In the minutes of the Waco Baptist Association from 1883 to 1899, Carroll's name is often found under a short report or listed as a speaker; however, no details are given (with the exception of the Martin Controversy). Perhaps the best and most concise report concerning Carroll's activity with the association during this time comes from J. L. Walker and C. P. Lumpkin, who state: "Brother Carroll has always been in active co-operation with all our organized work." Carroll himself, upon reviewing his tenure as the associational Mission Board chairman, stated that these years were "the most joyful and perhaps most successful service" of his life.[41]

CONSOLIDATION OF THE TEXAS CONVENTIONS

Organized Baptist work in Texas began on a statewide level in 1848 with the formation of the Baptist State Convention. This new body began to assist Baylor University, a Baptist school founded by the Education Committee of the Union Association three years earlier. The Baptist State Convention split five years after its inception, acreating a second organization. This second organization dissolved in 1868, then reformed as the Baptist General Association. This new body began to support another Baptist school in Texas, Waco University, which had been founded by former Baylor president Rufus C. Burleson in 1860. By the middle of the 1880s, therefore, Texas Baptists had two major statewide organizations with each supporting its own university. As J. M. Carroll states, the friction was becoming "acute and troublesome."[42]

In 1883 B. H. Carroll headed the first move toward consolidation. The Baptist General Association named him as chairman of a special committee to study its relationship to other Baptist groups in the state. In the committee's report, Carroll noted that there were five Baptist organizations in Texas:

> South of us lies the Baptist State Convention, a body older in organization than our own, one for which we cherish the profoundest love and respect for its glorious record of work in the Master's cause, in the many years of its history. To the east and along our northwest and western borders are respectively, the East Texas, North Texas and Central Texas Conventions, having in a great measure undefined and undefinable boundaries.[43]

After reviewing the difficulties that five separate bodies presented, Carroll's committee recommended that the association correspond with the other groups concerning unification. Three questions would be asked: "Is it desirable and expedient? Is it practicable? If so, under what form?"[44]

The overtures of Carroll's committee were not well-received by the Baptist State Convention, as revealed in Carroll's report to the 1884 meeting of the Baptist General Association concerning the progress of his committee's work:

> Your committee appointed to confer with like committees from the Baptist General bodies of this State . . . would submit that, after that reception given to our proposition by the Baptist State Convention at its last session in San Antonio, it was deemed best by the committee to take no further steps in the matter at present.[45]

Although consolidation discussions ended at this time, unification of the state bodies and talk of a consolidated university dominated the Baptist General Association meeting in July 1885. The association offered many resolutions concerning possible consolidation of the state bodies and of Waco and Baylor universities as well. The Baptist State Convention met later in the year and was more responsive to the association's overtures at that time. The convention appointed a committee to meet with Carroll and the association committee to explore the consolidation of Baylor and Waco universities.[46]

Committees from the Baptist General Association and Baptist State Convention met in Temple on December 9, 1885, with over fifty members present. After the group elected officers, Carroll, who had been on the nominating committee, moved that a subcommittee be appointed to "present a basis for consolidation of the schools." The group elected ten men, five from each body, including Carroll.[47]

The subcommittee met well into the night and on December 10 brought its report to the main body. Carroll spoke for the association, and C. R. Breedlove represented the convention. The subcommittee recommended in part:

1. That Waco and Baylor Universities be consolidated.
2. The name of the school shall be Baylor University.
3. That Baylor University be located at Waco, ...[48]

With the consolidation of the two schools complete, unification of the Baptist bodies soon followed. On December 10, 1885, the two groups merged to become the Baptist General Convention of Texas.

In July 1886, at the first annual meeting of the Baptist General Convention of Texas, Texas Baptists were seeking to consolidate their two newspapers. Although neither the *Texas Baptist Herald*, owned by J. B. Link, nor the *Texas Baptist*, owned by S. A. Hayden, was an official paper of the General Convention, many felt that a unified paper would serve Texas best. While Link and Hayden agreed on the need for a consolidated paper, they could not agree on its location — Link preferred Waco, and Hayden favored Dallas. After both men made their presentations, the convention decided to express its preference with a vote.[49]

Before messengers voted, Carroll stood and asked that Wacoans abstain. The Dallas messengers, however, did vote. The results indicated that Dallas had won 169 to 168. After a recount the margin was 177 to 174, again in favor of Dallas. Had the messengers from Waco voted, Waco likely would have been the site of the unified paper. Instead, Link sold the *Texas Baptist Herald* to Hayden, who moved the paper to Dallas and merged with the *Texas Baptist* to become the *Texas Baptist and Herald*. Waco messengers who abstained from the vote at the urging of Carroll not only cost the city a paper but also gave Hayden, a man who would soon be an opponent of Carroll, a powerful voice with which to speak.[50]

As consolidation work drew to a close, Carroll, whom the board of trustees had recently named as their president, stood with few others as a leader among Texas Baptists. Had the unified paper landed in Waco, the Baptist General Convention of Texas, which was heavily influenced by Carroll, might have been dominated by him. He would have been involved in shaping young Baptist minds through the university and older Baptist minds through the newspaper. In addition, his future rival — Hayden — would have been without an instrument to make his voice heard.

BAYLOR UNIVERSITY

From the beginning of Carroll's involvement with Baylor, ensuring the financial stability of the school was one of his top priorities. Soon after the consolidation with Waco University, Carroll urged that a financial agent be appointed. Baylor responded by assigning S. L. Morris to this position in 1887. Morris stayed for only a short time, and the university found itself facing a growing debt with the completion of Burleson Hall and Old Main. In Carroll's 1890 report concerning Baylor, he stated that the university had liabilities of $72,000. In an effort to wipe out the debt, Carroll put forth the following plan:

> We ask every Baptist preacher in Texas to raise from his church congregation or field, an average of $1.00 from each adult male member and 50 cents each from each female member or minor. That this be done by the first of January next. Let him appoint, where necessary, zealous canvassers to help him and on some suitable Sunday in December, take up a cash collection to round up all deficits. Let him send all funds thus collected directly to J. T. Battle, Secretary of Board of Trustees, stating number of church members.[51]

Because Baylor had been unsuccessful in keeping an agent on the field, the plan specified that churches should send their contributions directly to the secretary. Baylor mailed a circular letter announcing the plan to every pastor "whose address can be obtained."[52] On December 7, 1890, Carroll presented the plan to his own church. The minutes read:

> The pastor stated that he had mailed to every Baptist pastor in Texas a circular prepared by him as president of the board of trustees of Baylor University at Waco, in which he requested that they would raise from their respective churches one dollar from each adult male member, and 50 cents from each female and minor for the purpose of paying off the indebtedness of Baylor University, constructing another building, and making other much needed improvements.
>
> He said he greatly desired that this church would take the lead in this laudable effort. Thereupon it was moved and unanimously carried that this church indorse the plan and that the work of raising the money from the church be commenced next Sabbath.[53]

The church voted to release Carroll from his preaching duties for the month of December to allow him to work full-time on the campaign. Later the church allowed Carroll the freedom to be absent from the pulpit in the interest of Baylor University whenever necessary.

Baylor hired a new financial agent in 1891, a young minister who would later become one of the greatest preachers in the history of the Southern Baptist Convention. His name was George W. Truett. In the only surviving correspondence between Truett and Carroll concerning the financial campaign, Truett's dedication to his work is apparent:

> I cannot but daily weep at the dreadful indifference of pastors. The papers too, it seems to me, are practically against the work. . . . I hope to be able to present work Friday night, Sat. night and Sunday—will probably be at Farmerville Sunday. . . . It should be different, I cannot know. These brethren and sisters have endeared themselves to me as never before.[54]

According to Carroll's 1891 report to the convention, Truett had been on the field seven months; and Carroll, who once again had been given leave by First Baptist, had been on the field for three months. Together they raised $37,000 in cash, lands, and pledges.

As the campaign came to a close, Carroll and Truett discovered that they were still $800 short of their goal. Carroll told Truett that he would visit three men whom he believed would give $100 each to the campaign. While Carroll visited with these men, Truett went to see another whom he believed could help. Immediately after their visits, Carroll and Truett met. Carroll had the $300 that he had expected and asked Truett how much money he had collected. Truett stated that he had been able to collect the remaining $500 from his visit. They had reached the goal; and as the two men celebrated on the steps of First Baptist, Waco, Truett "cried like a child" out of joy and exhaustion.[55] Through the work of these two men, Baylor paid all debts for new buildings and grounds by 1893.[56]

One of the greatest contributions that Carroll made to Southern Baptists was his discovery of George W. Truett. During their campaign together the two men developed a close relationship which endured throughout Carroll's life. Upon completion of the campaign Truett enrolled at Baylor. Powhatan W. James describes Truett's relationship with Carroll during this time period:

> For six years George Truett had almost daily contact with his friend and teacher, Dr. B. H. Carroll. That in itself was a liberal education. He had free access to the Carroll private library which was one of the very best in the South. Dr. Carroll took delight in introducing his young friend to the great books on theology, history, literature, biography, philosophy, homiletics, Christian apologetics, Biblical criticism, and other subjects of special interest to an alert young preacher. Dr. Carroll was never happier than when talking to Truett far into the night on the great themes of religion, philosophy and literature. He gave to George Truett hundreds of hours of Socratic fellowship. He sought to lay solid foundations in the mind and heart of his protégé for the great work in life which he felt the young man would do. Student Truett never missed an opportunity to hear his teacher lecture, or converse, or preach.[57]

Interestingly, First Baptist Church, which in Carroll's early ministry insisted that he fill the pulpit regularly, allowed Carroll three extended leaves from 1890 to 1892 as well as the freedom to miss other Sundays, as he deemed necessary, in order to raise money for Baylor. Had Carroll not received this freedom, he no doubt would have threatened resignation and actually may have resigned. In the 1890s Carroll's role as president of the board of trustees at Baylor University quickly became as important to him as his role as pastor of First Baptist Church.

As Baylor's financial situation stabilized, Carroll and others recognized Baylor's need to find new leadership to carry her into the twentieth century. Rufus C. Burleson, Carroll's old mentor, had served as president of either Baylor or Waco universities since 1851. At the 1897 board of trustees meeting, many felt that the time had come for a change.

Two major factors contributed to this assessment — the Brann and Hayden Controversies. In 1895 Antonio Texeira, a Brazilian girl brought to Baylor by a missionary, was living in the Burleson home. Regulations of the school did not allow her to live in the girls' dormitory. During the time that Texeira was in the president's home, she became pregnant. Rumors began to circulate that Texeira had been raped by a Baylor student and that the Burlesons were trying to cover it up to protect the university. William C. Brann, publisher of a monthly paper called the *Iconoclast* and longtime critic of Baylor, began an attack on the university and Burleson. Brann stated that both school and president were "unworthy to have charge of female education and commend[ed] instead the convent schools under the direction of the Romish nuns."[58] Texeira was pregnant, but as a result of poor judgment not rape. Though Burleson could have done little to prevent the incident, the image of the school and president had been damaged. The question remained as to whether parents could be convinced to send their daughters to Baylor to live in the dormitory when they did not appear to be safe in the president's own home.

Carroll was unusually quiet during the controversy. In explaining his silence later, he said that he did not wish to get into a battle of words with Brann since so many of Brann's charges were false. Engaging in such a battle would only allow Brann to continue to "grind his axe" against Baylor. Despite Carroll's explanation, some believed that his silence was the first step in his plan to succeed Burleson. Keith Cogburn states that S. A. Hayden used this rumor to obtain Burleson's support for his own reforms.[59]

The second major factor which led to a reevaluation of Burleson's leadership was his stand in the Hayden Controversy (to be discussed in detail later). During the mid-1890s, S. A. Hayden began to attack the structure and leadership of the state convention. Burleson agreed with Hayden's calls for "reforms" in the Mission Board, an agreement which put him at odds with many prominent Baptist leaders, including his former student B. H. Carroll.[60]

At the board meeting on June 10, 1897, W. H. Jenkins introduced a resolution concerning Burleson's future at Baylor University. After some debate the Board passed a substitute motion which was similar to Jenkins' motion:

> Resolved, First, That Dr. R. C. Burleson be elected President Emeritus of Baylor University for life, on a salary of $2,000 per year, to be paid and received under all conditions of payment of professors doing regular class work.
> Resolved, Second, That the object of this election is not meant to sever his name, memory and influence from Baylor University, but relieving him of the duties and responsibilities of teaching and administration, onerous to his advanced age. Will allow him to do such general work of travel and correspondence and lecturing to young preachers as may suit his own convenience and inclination."[61]

Although no record exists of Carroll's speaking for the motion, it could not have passed without his full support. Burleson, who was reluctant to accept the appointment of president emeritus, did so to avoid severing ties with the school that he had served for forty-six years.[62] Rumors indicated that Carroll wanted Burleson's position; however, when the trustees attempted to name him as the next president, Carroll declined the offer.

Burleson became a fallen hero to Hayden, who honored him in the *Texas Baptist and Herald*.[63] In response to Hayden's editorials and to alumni upset with Burleson's dismissal, Carroll issued a statement on behalf of the trustees defending their decision. The lengthy statement explained the actions of the trustees and answered charges made by Hayden and others. The statement also documented that the trustees had the power to remove Burleson as president and showed that no law or agreement had been violated in doing so.[64]

Not all Texas Baptists were upset with the action of the board. In a letter to Carroll in September 1897, M. S. Pierson wrote:

> I commend the action of the Board of Trustees, in retiring Dr. Burleson, not that I love Dr. B. less, but Baylor University more. . . . I try to appreciate him for what he *has* done.

Addressing a call from Hayden that Carroll and the other trustees step down as a result of their actions, Pierson continued:

> I hope you will not entertain the thought for a moment, for if ever there was a time, when true and tried men were needed as Trustees of Baylor University, the time is now.[65]

Carroll and the other trustees weathered the storm. Though

the forced retirement of Burleson placed Carroll in an awkward position, he had to support the action to protect the school that he had worked to save from financial ruin. Carroll realized that with stable leadership at the university, fundraising would be easier. The question remains: Had Burleson not been involved in both the Brann and Hayden Controversies, would the trustees have replaced him?

During the 1890s, Baylor appointed Carroll, who was already chairman of the board of trustees at Baylor, to a faculty position with the responsibility of creating and directing a theological department from Baylor's rapidly growing theological contingency. (Carroll's involvement in this endeavor will be discussed in more detail in the next chapter.)

THE SOUTHERN BAPTIST CONVENTION

By the early 1880s, Carroll was becoming an active participator in and defender of the Southern Baptist Convention. When the Baptist General Convention of Texas considered a joint cooperation with the Home Mission Society of the Northern Baptists and the Home Mission Board of the Southern Baptist Convention, Carroll led the fight against such a dual alliance. He further "succeeded in committing Texas Baptists to the permanent policy of undivided cooperation with the Southern Board."[66] Carroll's stand on this issue no doubt endeared him to many Southern Baptist leaders in the East.

Robert A. Baker notes that "Carroll seems to have been a part of every concern of Southern Baptists . . . whether on the associational, the state, or the national level."[67] His greatest impact on the national level was in Home Missions, Sunday school, and theological education.

During the 1880s, some members of the Southern Baptist Convention spoke out against the Home Mission Board, saying it had served its purpose and should be abolished. Even after the major reorganization of the board in 1882, they still questioned the need for its existence. In 1888 Carroll addressed this issue in a speech entitled "In the Interest of the Home Mission Board and Vindicating its Appropriations to Texas," perhaps his most famous speech before the convention:

A Northern writer has said: "There are but two States in the American Union with a past rich enough in historic lore and romantic legend to furnish a theme for an epic poem grander than

the Illiad of Homer or the Eneid of Virgil. These States are Texas
and Virginia."

From one of them, the most western in the territory of the
Southern Baptist Convention, I come to-night for the first time in
life, to stand upon the soil of the other, the most eastern in our
bounds, to plead the cause of the Home Mission Board and to
vindicate the wisdom of its missionary operations.[68]

Carroll stated that the board should remain in existence if for
no other reason than to carry out work in the growing frontier of
Texas and in the Indian territories. The address had such an impact
on the convention that some who had planned to speak against the
board now spoke for it, and others did not speak at all. Ray states
that from that day forward, convention members did not question
the necessity of the Home Mission Board again.

While all historians who record Carroll's address credit him
with saving the Home Mission Board, none has highlighted the
other major point of his speech — that Texas deserved to be treated
as an equal partner with its Eastern brothers in the Southern Baptist
Convention. In noting the attitude of these older states, particularly
Virginia, Carroll stated:

> while your people come [to Texas], you keep your preachers back.
> I never was more amused than when reading the proceeding of
> your last State gathering and noticed how you exhausted all pos-
> sible expedients to keep Virginia preachers at home. Your reports
> were wonderfully doleful and lugubrious. But you hesitated not in
> the meantime to reach out to all lands and to cull the excellent of
> the earth to supply your Richmond pulpits. And with your good
> people you also sent to Texas shores every ecclesiastical crotchet,
> every tangled theological hand (no allusion to the Dallas pastor),
> made and bred from Dismal and Okefinokee [sic] swamps to the
> lagoons of Louisiana.[69]

Though Texas was a frontier state, Carroll clearly resented its
being viewed as a theological dumping ground. This theme of re-
specting Texas Baptists as well as Baptists throughout the Southwest would later become the cornerstone of Carroll's position in the
Whitsitt Controversy.

Carroll addressed the Southern Baptist Convention again in
1906 about the establishment of a Department of Evangelism. The
new department was controversial, and the convention's endorsement of it was uncertain. Carroll affirmed the report calling for its

creation and requested the convention to do likewise. His eloquent address expressed his support for basic evangelism and called for the formation of the Evangelism Department. After his speech, the report was adopted with only a few dissenting votes.

In 1910 Carroll began to support the plan to expand the convention from a regional to a national denomination. In an article appearing in many Baptist papers, he stated:

> It would be disastrous and suicidal for our Convention which represents more than half the Baptists of the world, to gratuitously build an unscalable wall around itself and construct a dam across the outflowing stream of its operations. This would be to brand ourselves as sectional, to subvert our own constitution to repudiate sound Baptist polity, and to arbitrarily and sinfully divest ourselves of responsibility for the evangelization of this ever-enlarging Nation. Even a shell-fish must die that can neither enlarge its shell as it grows, nor has sense enough to crawl out of a shell that will not expand.[70]

Carroll stated that he would be willing to send Southern Baptist aid to anyone in the nation who requested it. Some Southerners, however, were too deeply scarred to allow any Northern participation in the convention. In recognition of their feelings Carroll closed by saying: "If, when there was a sectional North and a sectional South we used to shoot at each other, I am now willing to stand in line with them and shoot spiritual guns only at the enemies of our Lord."[71]

Historians who have recorded Carroll's work within the Southern Baptist Convention credit him with playing a pivotal role in the creation of the Sunday School Board. Jeff D. Ray writes:

> Nobody who knows the inside history of that Board is ignorant of the vital part he played in its founding. Nobody familiar with the facts doubts that J. M. Frost would have found it exceedingly difficult, if not absolutely impossible, to carry through the Convention his proposition for the establishment of this Board, when the matter was fought out in Fort Worth in 1890, had it not been for the influence and golden-mouthed advocacy of B. H. Carroll. He was a member of the committee to which the matter was referred by the Convention. The committee could not agree, and brought in a minority and majority report. His speech had much to do with the adoption of the majority report.[72]

Little evidence exists to show the extent of Carroll's influence in the founding of the Sunday School Board. Given his earlier speech for the Home Mission Board, he doubtlessly had some impact; but to say, however, that Frost might have found it "impossible" to establish the board if not for Carroll is to give Carroll too much credit.

Carroll's role in theological education in the Southern Baptist Convention, aside from the founding of Southwestern Seminary, was highlighted by his service on the board of trustees of Southern Baptist Theological Seminary from 1894 until 1911. During his tenure, he was a major participant in the Whitsitt Controversy. Aside from that controversy possibly the most interesting aspect of his service as a trustee of Southern was that from 1908 until 1911 he was also president of Southwestern. Though few people spoke out concerning this conflict of interest, apparently fundraising for Southern in Texas was difficult.[73]

During the latter half of Carroll's ministry, he had truly become a national leader. Based on his own correspondence, many people sought his opinions and advice on issues within the convention. While one might argue with Sampey's statement citing Carroll as the leader of the Southern Baptist Convention after Broadus' death, the fact that Carroll's name is mentioned with Broadus' shows his prominence in the convention.

CONTROVERSIES

M. T. Martin

The controversy involving Matthew Thomas (M. T.) Martin apparently took Carroll by surprise. Martin had come to Texas in the early 1880s. Although he had no theological training, he considered himself a theologian. In fact, Martin saw the absence of theological training as a benefit because he was not bound by the "bands of tradition" that burdened other ministers.[74] Martin traveled throughout the state preaching revivals and expounding upon his unique view of theology.

The first significant event involving Martin occurred in December 1884, when A. T. Hawthorne, a well-known minister, was converted, rebaptized, and reordained by Martin.[75] Soon Martin was asked to explain his "new thoughts on old theology."[76] He did this with a series of three articles in March 1885, which appeared in the *Texas Baptist Herald*. Though much of what Martin wrote differed

M. T. Martin, leader of Martinism.
— Courtesy Southwestern Baptist Theological Seminary Archives

from traditional Baptist views, a theological debate was put on hold as Texas became involved in the prohibition campaign and the move toward consolidation of its Baptist state organizations.

Martin, who was still actively teaching his views throughout the state, joined the First Baptist Church of Waco in 1886 almost without notice. Carroll was aware of Martin's unique theological views, but he apparently saw no reason for concern. Carroll and Martin developed a casual friendship and supposedly "agreed to disagree" on their doctrinal differences including Martin's belief that those truly saved would never doubt their salvation.[77] This accepting relationship between the two men was very unusual, given Carroll's concern for orthodoxy. Had Carroll known the full extent of Martin's teachings, he probably would not have "agreed to disagree." Perhaps Carroll was busy with consolidation and prohibition, or perhaps his judgment was clouded by his relationship with Martin. Whatever Carroll's reasons for remaining silent, he handled the early days of the controversy in a way that was very unlike himself.

In 1887, with consolidation finished and prohibition defeated, questions concerning Martin's theology began to resurface. S. A. Hayden expressed concern over the large number of rebaptisms under Martin's ministry and asked Martin to write on rebaptism for the *Texas Baptist and Herald*. Martin agreed, and J. B. Link became his adversary in a newspaper debate. As a result of Link's sharp attacks on his theology, Martin began to publish a monthly theological journal to better explain his positions. In the introduction to his journal, Martin admitted that his ideas might be controversial:

> This journal will as its title indicates, take the Gospel, as revealed, as the STANDARD, and acknowledge nothing of later origin, whatever may be its pretensions, as a rule of faith and practice, or a guide to thought and expression. . . .
>
> In the editorials of the STANDARD there may be found enunciations, which at first glance may be thought to be heterodox, and they *may be heterodox* when *compared with standards which men have erected*, yet, upon careful examination they may be found orthodox when compared with the STANDARD — the word of God. Do not jump at conclusions, brethren. Do not presume that we are going astray, but give us a patient hearing; and then, if need be, criticise in the spirit of Christian kindness.[78]

As the debate began to rage between pro- and anti-Martin forces, Carroll quietly entered the controversy by counseling Martin to keep a low profile until the debate calmed down. Martin, however, was benefiting from the controversy; and by the end of 1888 he had weathered the assaults of his accusers and continued to gain converts to his position.[79] Texas Baptists needed their champion to dual this feisty challenger.

On January 28, 1889, A. J. Holt, superintendent of missions and corresponding secretary of the Baptist General Convention of Texas, wrote to Carroll asking him to write a "thorough review" of Martin for the *Texas Baptist and Herald*:

> . . . you are looked upon as being thoroughly conversant with all phases of our faith, and as you are at the seat of our University, and the pastor of Bro. Martin, all these thing *[sic]* make it expedient that you should write this review. It will be criminal should we sit idly by while he goes on perfecting his plans to divide and destroy our denominational institutions, and our most cherished doctrines. Somebody must meet him, and I verily believe that "thou art the man."[80]

Carroll apparently was still not ready to publicly enter the debate; however, after a plea from S. A. Hayden, on February 4 he agreed. Carroll's article "Bro. Carroll Reviews Bro. Martin" appeared in the *Herald* on February 13. Carroll offered no explanation for his delay in writing on the subject, although he did admit to being uncomfortable publicly assessing the theology of a member of his church. From the tone of the article Carroll clearly saw Martin as no serious threat. Carroll addressed Martin's theology as the product of an undisciplined child rather than a theologian. The real threat of the controversy to Carroll was that it could lead to a breakup of the three-year-old Baptist General Convention of Texas if it did not end.[81]

Martin, hurt and humiliated by the way Carroll treated him in the article, responded the next week by stating boldly that he was not afraid to debate Carroll. He went on to say:

> There seems to be the idea in the heads of a few men that there is a kind of something called the "denomination" represented by a very few men who must be consulted and whose word is law. . . .
>
> There is creeping out a species of denominational bossism which is injurious in tendency; . . . Baptists will not be bossed by a vague something called a denomination.[82]

Martin continued by telling his opponents that they would live to regret their attacks on him if the criticism did not cease.[83]

Carroll, no doubt one of the denominational bosses to whom Martin referred, did not react kindly to the veiled threats. Acting as a man who had just had his nose bloodied by a former friend, Carroll called Martin before the deacons for an examination of his theology. Unable to identify any heresy, the deacons adjourned. But while Carroll reported to Texas Baptists that the matter was over, he continued to search for more evidence against Martin.[84]

On March 22, 1889, Carroll sent questionnaires to pastors throughout the state:

> DEAR BROTHER: — As doubtless you are aware, there is some concern in our church about Bro. M. T. Martin. His membership is here, and, therefore, this church is justly responsible for his ministerial teachings and practices.
>
> His labor in Texas, while holding membership with us, has been almost exclusively elsewhere. As an evangelist, he has held meetings in very many places. Hence, our knowledge of him must be derived mainly from the reports of others. These reports are conflicting, and hence embarrass us. We are informed that you have had opportunity to judge of his preaching and work, . . . Will you, in the interest of truth, frankly answer the following questions. We want no confidential letters that we can not read to the church.[85]

After the respondents returned the questionnaires, Carroll was provided with the evidence that he needed. On July 14 Martin, aware that he was no longer welcome and perhaps aware of the circulating questionnaire, requested a letter of dismissal in good standing. Though that motion was made, a substitute motion calling for a church trial to be held against Martin on the charge of heresy passed.[86]

The four-day trial opened on July 17 with a reading of the general charges against Martin:

> Rev. M. T. Martin, member and ordained minister of this Church, has at various places and times since his connection with this Church and responsibility to it, taught doctrines contrary to our acknowledged standards of faith and polity, thereby causing division and troubles in our denomination. . . .
>
> And we further charge that even in so short a time in certain places where his doctrines have been received and his spirit imbibed the effect had been detrimental to prayer-meetings, sunday-schools, mission-work, and other denominational activities.[87]

Martin was charged with teaching doctrine contrary to both the

New Hampshire and Philadelphia Confessions of Faith on regeneration, sanctification, faith, assurance, and repentance, as well as false teaching concerning prayer.

Carroll and the deacons of the church convinced the congregation of Martin's guilt and by a thirty-two to eleven vote, recalled his credentials as a minister. Some church members then moved to withdraw fellowship from Martin, but at the urging of Carroll that motion was dropped, and Martin was dismissed as a member in good standing.[88]

Opponents of Martin openly questioned how First Baptist could find him guilty of heresy and yet consider Martin to be a member in "good standing."[89] Perhaps Carroll made the motion for "good standing" in hope that the controversy would soon fade or that by dismissing Martin he would become another pastor's problem. Unfortunately if this is what Carroll had hoped for, he was wrong.

After his dismissal Martin moved to Georgia for a short period of time before returning to Texas. In the summer of 1889 H. H. Tucker sent Carroll an ominous warning: "I understand that Martin is now in Texas and that his object is to get himself reinstated to the ministry."[90] In September, Martin united with the First Baptist Church of Marlin, where J. R. M. Touchstone, the pastor, warmly received him.

The Marlin church contacted Carroll and the people of First Baptist to inquire if First Baptist would reinstate the ministerial credentials of Martin. Carroll formed a selected committee to consider the request on December 8, 1889. He saw Martin's return to the Waco Association as a direct challenge to the authority of the Waco church. The request from the Marlin church was denied.[91] Touchstone saw Carroll's tactics as heavy handed and believed that a majority of the Waco church favored reinstating Martin. Considering the fact that five months earlier the congregation would have revoked Martin's membership had not Carroll intervened, Touchstone's assumption was wrong.

Setting the stage for a fiery associational meeting, Touchstone and the Marlin church restored Martin's credentials over the objections of the Waco church. Carroll successfully led a campaign to have the Marlin church excluded for violating a number of articles of the associational constitution by reinstating Martin over the objections of First Baptist. A year later, after Martin had returned to Georgia, Marlin was readmitted to the Association after Touchstone made a brief apology.[92]

Though Martin was gone, Martinism was not. Considered to be the Martin expert, Carroll received correspondence throughout the 1890s from people concerned about Martinism and its ministerial followers.[93] In 1895 the Waco Association, citing continued confusion and concern over Martinism, urged all Baptist bodies to dismiss anyone who still followed Martin's teachings. In the same year the state convention passed a resolution rejecting as a messenger anyone who believed or taught Martinism.[94]

Carroll's role in the Martin Controversy is at best confusing. Reluctant to enter, he tried to end the debate by slapping Martin on the hand, only to be slapped in the face. Insulted by Martin's response, Carroll worked to remove him from his church but allowed him to be dismissed in good standing. Had the Waco church revoked Martin's membership, the later conflict with the Marlin church may have been avoided. Carroll's reaction to the Marlin church clearly showed that he did not like to be challenged. As a result of the Martin Controversy, regardless of the mistakes he may have made in the way it was handled, Carroll emerged stronger in the eyes of many and as a clear defender of orthodoxy among Baptists.

The Hayden Controversy

The controversy involving S. A. Hayden and the Baptist General Convention of Texas is often recorded as beginning in 1894; however, the actual roots of the controversy occurred years earlier. Soon after the consolidation of the two Baptist state papers, disenchantment arose over the way Hayden was using the paper to attack his critics. As a result of this displeasure, in 1888 Lewis Holland founded an alternative Baptist paper, the *Baptist News,* in Honey Grove. The paper's circulation was small, with most of the subscribers living in East Texas. R. T. Hanks purchased the paper in 1890, renamed it the *Western Baptist,* and began to work toward circulating the paper statewide. In 1892 M. V. Smith and J. B. Cranfill, who was well-known through his paper the *Waco Advance,* bought the *Western Baptist.* The men quickly moved the operation to Waco and changed the name of the paper to the *Texas Baptist Standard.*[95] As displeasure with the *Baptist and Herald* grew, the subscription list of the *Standard* increased.

When the *Standard* continued to flourish, Hayden took notice. Feeling betrayed by the leadership of the Baptist General Convention of Texas, he often attacked the publication, seeing it as a violation of the consolidation agreement of 1886. In November 1890, Hayden enlisted Carroll to write an article concerning the two papers. At this time Carroll supported Hayden's contention that there need be only one Baptist paper in Texas, although he did not fully endorse Hayden as its leader. Carroll recommended that the two papers merge into a "joint stock company" so that control would not rest with one man.[96] The *Western Baptist* was shocked by Carroll's article and could not believe that he would write such a statement given the fact that only months before Hayden had referred to Carroll as a "confused" man.[97] Although Carroll did write the article for Hayden, tension was evident between the two men. In July, Hayden wrote to Carroll assuring him that he was not spreading rumors about Carroll's first marriage. From the tone of the letter Carroll evidently had accused Hayden of trying to damage his reputation. In writing the article, Carroll, who over the last five years had dealt with consolidation, prohibition, and Martinism, was simply trying to keep the peace.[98]

Hope for a quiet resolution did not last long. When Carroll's friend and church member J. B. Cranfill bought the *Standard* in 1892, Carroll allowed Cranfill to publish his Sunday morning sermons in the paper. This venture proved to be a successful drawing card for the young paper.

In response Hayden contacted Carroll about publishing his Sunday evening sermons in the *Baptist and Herald*. Wishing to show no favoritism, Carroll agreed. The plan quickly developed problems, however, because the presence of Hayden's stenographer hindered Carroll's extemporaneous delivery, a style he adapted on Sunday nights. Carroll also felt that he did not have adequate time to correct the manuscripts. Therefore he asked Hayden to release him from their agreement.[99] Hayden maintained that Cranfill had influenced Carroll to withdraw in an effort to damage the *Baptist and Herald*.[100]

In January 1894, fire destroyed the press of the *Standard*. Cranfill immediately sent out a plea for advance subscriptions which would allow the paper to begin printing once again. Money came in from across the state, as well as the nation, from people such as Robert Burdette and John A. Broadus.[101] One of those to send in a five dollar subscription was J. M. Carroll, brother of B. H. Carroll and corresponding secretary of the board of directors of the Baptist General Convention of Texas. When J. M.'s name appeared on a list of subscribers, Hayden believed that it would appear as a denominational endorsement of the *Standard*.[102] He was convinced that many of the leadership of the Baptist General Convention of Texas wanted to see his paper ruined. With the attitude that it was he against the Baptist General Convention of Texas, Hayden addressed a letter to the members of the board, of which he was a member, to be discussed at their next meeting.

When the board gathered in April, they discussed Hayden's letter in which he cited the board's excessive expenses, increasing debts, decreasing missionaries, and the overly generous salary of the board's secretary, J. M. Carroll. Hayden stated that he would push for reform in the board's mission work. B. H. Carroll quickly made a motion for Hayden to detail his proposed reform and also stated for the record that the board did not operate in secret, a charge levied by Hayden. In response, Hayden detailed the accusations made in his letter yet offered no specific reforms. The board named a committee of five to investigate the charges which they found to be groundless. In an interesting move, Hayden himself made the motion that the committee's report be accepted. In an effort to lessen the damage caused by Hayden's charges, B. H. Carroll presented the following resolution:

> Resolved, that the privations and sufferings of our missionaries to which references have been made in our pulpits and newspapers, are in no wise due or attributable to any act or omission of this board, but wholly due to continued drouths and other local conditions in their several fields, rendering the local brethren and churches unable to make their usual contributions for their support.
>
> The corresponding secretary and all other helpers in their appeals for mission money were strenuously urging the largest possible mission contributions, in part because of local conditions in the fields where the missionaries were at work. These local fields, because of drouth, and other local conditions, were falling down on the part they were to pay to the missionary. Hence the urgent necessity for our board to pay its part promptly and fully. And it was doing that, even though it had to borrow the money. That policy then adopted by the board has been strictly adhered to ever since.[103]

After the April meeting, Hayden continued his call for change and eventually found his reform program in the writings of T. P. Crawford. Crawford, a disciple of J. R. Graves, believed that there was no need for mission boards and that churches should support missionaries directly. Hayden began echoing this belief in the *Bap-*

tist and Herald and pointed to the debt of the current Mission Board as an example of why it should be disbanded.[104] Interestingly, at that April meeting Hayden had no specific reform program; but with the help of Crawford's teachings, he was able to formulate one. Whether Hayden actually believed Crawford's principles or merely used them as a means of attack against the board is subject to question.

As a result of Hayden's continued criticism, the board met again in June. At the meeting the announcement was made that First Baptist, Waco, and First Baptist, Dallas, had given their pastors, B. H. Carroll and George W. Truett, three months' leave from their churches to concentrate on one of the areas that Hayden was attacking — the board's debt. The two men were successful; and by the time of the state convention in Marshall in October 1894, the debt no longer existed.[105]

At the Marshall convention evidence indicated that support for Hayden's message was growing not only among the general population people but also among members of the Mission Board. In an effort to acknowledge the different opinions on the board concerning Hayden, yet at the same time end the controversy, the board included the following paragraph in its report:

> 2. That it is the duty of the minority of the board to acquiesce in the action of the majority on all matters coming before it, and if dissatisfied with such action, to appeal to the Convention at its next annual session after having given due notice of such appeal in open board meeting, and that pending such appeal no agitation of the matters at issue should be carried on in the public prints or otherwise.[106]

Hayden, as the report called for, remained quiet on the controversy in 1895. On January 23, 1896, however, he quickly rekindled the fire in an article entitled "Centralization." Hayden warned in the article of the danger of power in the hands of a few, such as the Mission Board, and how such power could ruin the denomination.[107] Carroll did not immediately respond, perhaps hoping that if he remained silent the controversy would remain dormant. When evidence indicated that Hayden would awaken the controversy with or without Carroll, Carroll responded with his patience gone and his opinion clear. Stating that Hayden and his followers had "no honest business in the Baptist General Convention of Texas," Carroll invited them to leave. Carroll believed that each member of the convention should support its work. He stated that according to the convention's constitution, "members from no church . . . failing to cooperate, can lawfully claim a seat in this body."[108]

The battle lines for the 1896 convention in Houston were drawn — if Hayden could not cooperate he should not be a messenger. The 1896 convention was an interesting time for Carroll; for while he was in the midst of the Hayden Controversy, the Whitsitt Controversy, in which he would be an active participant, loomed on the horizon. The Mission Board, by a vote of thirty-two to six, recommended that Hayden not be seated. After four days of debate, the convention voted to seat Hayden but also to censure him.

With his partial victory at the 1896 convention, Hayden used a large portion of the *Baptist and Herald* to attack Carroll and other men who opposed him. Hayden also predicted a clear victory for his forces at the 1897 convention. Burleson's removal as president of Baylor University at this time added to the controversy. While the Burleson issue gave Hayden new followers, his continued attacks upon Carroll, long seen by many as a champion of the Baptist faith, alienated others who before had been neutral in the controversy.

With the convention expected to be the largest in its short history, Weatherford, the meeting site, withdrew its sponsorship of the event because of lack of accommodations.[109] Many Hayden supporters resided in this area of the state, and the change of sites was clearly a blow to his movement. Interestingly, Carroll was in Weatherford at the time of the vote. While no evidence exists that Carroll influenced the vote, his presence in the town probably affected the outcome.[110]

Though the 1897 convention, now meeting in San Antonio, would be a decisive one, Carroll did not attend — his wife was dying. At the convention W. H. Jenkins, one of Carroll's faithful deacons, blamed Hayden for her death. He then asked: "Are you going to turn this man loose without a rebuke for the scars he has put on this dead woman's heart?"[111] After two days of debate the convention voted 582 to 104 not to seat Hayden.

Hayden filed a libel suit in 1898 against thirty-three Texas Baptist leaders, including B. H. Carroll, as a result of his exclusion from the 1897 convention. The courts tried the case six times with no verdict; Carroll himself testified on numerous occasions. Finally, in 1905 J. B. Cranfill settled the suit by secretly giving Hayden money from his own pocket in an attempt to end the controversy. With the suit settled, "Hayden confronted the beginning of his end as a factor in the Life of Texas Baptists."[112]

Hayden tried to be seated at the 1898, 1899, and 1900 conventions without success.[113] After the 1900 meeting he took Carroll's advice from years earlier and left the convention completely to join a group of his followers in forming the Baptist Missionary Association. From 1900 to 1911 a number of churches left the Baptist General Convention of Texas to join the new group.[114]

Hayden's real fight was not over the conducting of the mission effort but was actually a personal vendetta against a group of men who he believed were trying to decrease his influence among Texas Baptists by weakening his newspaper. The only way for Hayden to attack these men was by attacking the denominational structures which they led. Carroll counterattacked in an attempt to protect the unity of the convention. By 1896 Carroll perceived Haydenism as a cancer among Texas Baptists — the longer he stayed in the body, the more damage he would do. In a sense Carroll's fight against Hayden can be seen as the work of a denominational surgeon. Although he realized that some of the body would be lost when Hayden was removed, Carroll knew that if Hayden were allowed to stay, the body might die.

CARROLL AND THEOLOGY

Carroll was not a theologian in the same sense as James P. Boyce or J. R. Graves; he could more aptly be described as a "religious thinker." Carroll assimilated the views of many theologians into his own theology. Although not a theologian in the classical sense, Carroll's interpretation of doctrinal issues was considered the final word by many people. Many of Carroll's written works concerning his view of basic doctrinal issues did not appear until after his death, however.[115]

Since neither the Southern Baptist Convention nor any Texas Baptist group of which Carroll was a member issued a confession during his lifetime, Carroll used the New Hampshire Confession as his guide.[116] This Confession was only a guide because the cornerstone of Carroll's theology was the inspired and revealed word of God as illustrated in *Inspiration of the Bible*. Published after his death from a series of lectures that he delivered, this collection clearly articulates Carroll's view that the Bible was the verbally inspired word of God. Carroll reasoned that the Bible was verbally inspired because there was no other way to communicate ideas except through words.[117]

During the middle 1800s a theological movement arose among Baptists in response to the Campbellites who were overtaking many frontier Baptist churches. Landmarkism, as the movement became know, emphasized that the Baptist church was the true church and that each local church was autonomous. As a result of their beliefs Landmarkists attempted to redirect the responsibility of the missions effort from the convention to each local church. Based on Carroll's views of the church and Baptist history, some have tied him to this theological system.

Landmark theology undoubtedly influenced Carroll. Upon opening a series of lectures on *Pendleton's Church Manual*, he stated: "When I was a boy the great Baptist trio of the South was J. M. Pendleton, J. R. Graves, and A. C. Dayton."[118] These three men were the major leaders of the Landmark movement. Baker notes that after Graves visited Texas during the Baptist State Convention in 1859, "Texas Baptists were never quite the same."[119] Carroll did have some personal contact with Graves, but the extent of that contact is unknown.

Carroll's view of the church was similar in many respects to Graves' view. Both agreed that the church was the local body of believers. The time-church, as Carroll referred to it, was the visible, local church; there was no invisible, universal church on earth.[120] Though Carroll supported Graves' view of the church, he rejected Graves' belief that the kingdom of God and churches of Christ were synonymous.[121] Carroll believed that the kingdom of God was broader than a simple gathering of churches.[122] He was not as strict as Graves was on the issue of closed communion. And his eschatological beliefs were different from Graves' beliefs as well — Carroll was a postmillennialist and Graves was a premillennialist.[123]

Their strongest area of agreement was on the subject of Baptist church successionism. Both Carroll and Graves affirmed that Baptist churches had existed from the "days of John the Baptist."[124] If Baptist history was their strongest area of agreement, then Baptist missions was their strongest area of disagreement. Carroll, an ardent supporter of Baptist missions work, would never have agreed with Graves' 1859 statement concerning the Foreign Mission Board:

> There are elements at work that threaten the disruption of the relation of the convention and the Foreign Board to the body of the Southern Baptists. There are schemes of consolidation and centralization now urged by certain brethren who exercise a con-

trolling influence in the Biennial Convention which, if they succeed in consummating, will as certainly destroy the present union of Southern Baptists in Foreign Missions as the Convention meets in May next. And there is a determination on the part of some, moved more by partizan than missionary zeal, to make the next Biennial Convention an ecclesiastical Court and to force its decision into antagonism with Churches and Associations.[125]

Graves' argument was similar to S. A. Hayden's argument, which Carroll opposed in the 1890s. All of the missions-related movements that arose out of Landmarkism were opposed by Carroll. In fact the only movement that Carroll did support which had Landmark influences was the Whitsitt Controversy; and although that controversy dealt with successionism, it was only a secondary issue for Carroll.

Carroll did share some theological and historical views with the Landmarkists, but there were too many areas of disagreement to consider him a true Landmarker. Carroll's support of the denominational board system and his campaign against Landmarkist movements that threatened that system also separated him from Landmarkism.

If Carroll is labeled a Landmarker because of his doctrinal view of the church, then one must differentiate between the Landmarkism of Carroll and the Landmarkism of Graves. Carroll would be seen as a "denominational Landmarker," denoting his loyalty to the board system. To include Carroll among Landmarkers without special notation, however, is akin to insisting that all who believe in justification by faith are Lutheran.

CONTINUED MINISTRY AT
FIRST BAPTIST CHURCH, WACO

During the latter half of Carroll's ministry at First Baptist, Waco, the church continued to grow. In 1884 it reported a total membership of 424. By the end of Carroll's ministry the congregation numbered close to 1,000.[126] First Baptist started several mission churches during Carroll's pastorate, including Columbus Avenue Baptist Church and Seventh and James Baptist Church. First Baptist also earned a reputation as a strong financial supporter of Texas Baptist missions, as one-tenth of all money raised for Texas Baptist work from 1880 to 1890 came from this congregation. In 1884 the church paid the full salary of S. F. Sparks, the financial agent for Buckner Orphans' Home.[127] Under Carroll's leadership, First Baptist truly became the flagship church of Texas Baptists and one of the most prominent congregations in the Southern Baptist Convention.

Although Carroll's tenure was successful overall, it was not without its problems. In a move that took many church members by surprise, Carroll submitted his resignation at the February 1887 business conference of the church. The text of the resignation did not appear in the minutes, but from the clerk's account it appeared to be based on two factors. First, Carroll was criticized for neglecting the church during his work in the prohibition campaign, even though the church had released him from his duties at the time. Second, the church, once again, was considerably behind in paying the pastor's salary.[128]

As with the 1877 resignation, the church accepted this latest offer and then immediately elected Carroll pastor once again. A committee met with Carroll after the conference urging him to stay and promising to pay his back salary within thirty days. At the next conference in March, Carroll informed the church that his concerns had been addressed and that he would continue as their pastor.[129] Carroll's time away from the church was never again questioned, and on many occasions the church released him from his duties to allow him to carry out denominational responsibilities. In addition, the church would never be late in paying Carroll's salary again. As the 1890s approached, First Baptist seemed to be keenly aware of the role that its pastor played at both the state and national levels and of the resulting status that he brought to their church. As a result Carroll usually received whatever he desired from the church, and by mid-1895 his salary was $2,500 annually.[130]

In September 1893, the recently formed Baptist Young People's Union asked Carroll to call for a revival in the church. The church immediately agreed, and Carroll decided to preach the revival himself. For the next eight weeks Carroll preached day and night as many of the most prominent people in Waco joined the church. In recalling the event, W. H. Jenkins wrote:

> One of the main features of this revival was the fact that it was carried out without the aid of an evangelist. Dr. Carroll, himself, preached two sermons a day throughout the meeting, except for three days when he was ill. During this absence George W. Truett, one of the elders of the church, did the preaching.

Though hundreds were converted and one hundred and seventy-three additions were made to the church during the revival of 1893, these were not the greatest results. The influence of the meeting was felt in every church in the city. People talked about the revival on the streets, in stores, in the slums, in the surrounding country, in distant parts of the state, and even in other states. Letters came from other cities and other states asking for special prayer. No case was too hard or too far off for the faith of this church, for they were a "willing people."[131]

As a result of the revival the church quickly outgrew its auditorium. Burkhalter believes that the revival would have been even greater if the auditorium had held more. To provide extra room for future revivals, the church constructed a tabernacle in the summer of 1895. This tabernacle remained in use for various occasions until a new sanctuary was completed in 1908.[132] Though Carroll enjoyed his work at First Baptist, by the late 1890s his dual jobs at Baylor — trustee and dean — began to demand more and more of his time. Eventually, Carroll would have to choose between his work as an educator and his work as a minister.

CARROLL'S RESIGNATION
FROM FIRST BAPTIST CHURCH, WACO

The fall of 1897 brought a shocking change to Carroll's life. As he prepared to lead the convention fight against Hayden, Ellen Bell, his wife of thirty-two years, became ill and died on November 5. This loss devastated Carroll. In a letter to T. T. Eaton, Carroll permitted a rare glimpse into his inner emotions:

> On the 5th of November came the blow which *stunned* me. And for more than two months I have remained stunned. One month of the time — far away in the wood and prairies. . . . I am not yet able to take hold of anything. Least of all to write about my loss — overwhelming and irreparable in time.
>
> It seems a shoreless ocean rolls between me and all things which occurred prior to the 5th of November. I have not one atom of despair — not one rebellious thought — not one horror in regard to death, on the contrary absolute submission and faith and hope — only this is my problem: I have no desire — no will to recross that intervening and shoreless tide and take up again what seems the affairs of a bygone-world.[133]

Carroll asked the congregation at First Baptist to pray that he would recapture his desire. J. M., however, believed that it was time for Carroll to use his talents full-time to strengthen the Education Commission of the Baptist General Convention of Texas. By the end of 1898 Carroll agreed. On January 1, 1899, exactly twenty-eight years after First Baptist had called him as pastor, Carroll stood to read his resignation. This time there would be no concessions by the church nor special committees formed to keep the pastor. This time Carroll's resignation would be accepted.

In the resignation Carroll noted that during his ministry there had never been "a church trouble." Apparently, the M. T. Martin affair had little effect on the membership of First Baptist. Carroll also stated that he never asked the church to enter into any "enterprise without taking the lead," and the church always did what he asked of it. Carroll, of course, omits the fact that on three occasions he resigned before getting the church's cooperation. Finally, Carroll "rejoiced" in the status that the church had obtained under his leadership. As a result of Carroll's leadership in the church, as well as his prominence in Baptist affairs, by 1899 First Baptist, Waco, truly was the flagship church in Texas. The church received Carroll's resignation "sorrowfully and with many tears."[134] Although his pastorate at First Baptist Church had ended, the major work of Carroll's life had just begun.

CHAPTER 4

The Educator

EARLY INVOLVEMENT IN MINISTERIAL EDUCATION

After being licensed and ordained to the ministry by Caldwell Baptist Church in 1866, B. H. Carroll preached in many churches in the area. Robert Baker notes that Carroll's first published words were in the *Texas Baptist Herald*, January 16, 1867, when Carroll reported the results of a revival that he had led.[1] In 1867 Carroll conducted a revival at Spring Hill, about ten miles south of Waco. His preaching evidently was well received, for in 1869 New Hope Baptist Church, located near Spring Hill, called him as pastor.

Carroll's tenure at New Hope would be brief, for shortly after his arrival events began that would lead him to the pastorate of First Baptist, Waco. In the spring of 1869 Rufus Burleson, who was president of Waco University, asked Carroll to deliver the commencement address at the school. Later that year, Carroll led a revival at First Baptist Church, Waco. When the church became pastorless in the fall of 1869, Burleson agreed to become its minister and called Carroll to be his assistant. A few months later, when Burleson asked to be relieved of his responsibilities, the church extended a call to Carroll to become the full-time pastor. Carroll accepted, and for the next twenty-eight years he would have almost daily contact with the ministerial students at the university in Waco.[2]

Ministerial students at Baylor University in 1895.
— Courtesy Southwestern Baptist Theological Seminary Archives

WACO/BAYLOR UNIVERSITY

Carroll became active in the life of Waco University soon after accepting the job as assistant to Burleson at First Baptist. He delivered two addresses at the university in 1870.³ Carroll's support for the school and for ministerial education is seen in his first recorded public statement on education found in the 1871 Minutes of the Waco Association. Carroll, listed as chairman for a report on "School and Education," stated:

> Waco University is now ten years old. It matriculated 244 students last year. It has educated and otherwise assisted fifteen young ministers, besides much gratuitous instruction to preachers' children, and orphans of Confederate dead. It has ever been under the efficient presidency of Rev. R. C. Burleson, D.D.
> ... Your committee recommends to this Association the immediate necessity of helping in some practical, tangible way, this University.⁴

The exact date that Carroll began to give personal attention and instruction to ministerial students is unknown, though Jeff D. Ray records that Carroll was instructing young ministers as far back as 1873. Scholars believe that William Buck Bagby, a well-known missionary, was Carroll's first ministerial student. Helen Harrison, Bagby's daughter, says that Bagby often recalled his role in the enterprise which developed into Southwestern Seminary: "Yes, Dr. Carroll and I founded the seminary. He was the faculty and I was the student body."⁵

By 1880 Carroll was leading what Ray calls an "embryonic theological seminary" in connection with the university. This "class" consisted of fifteen young ministers and was held on Friday nights in Carroll's home. *Pendleton's Church Manual* was the textbook for the course. Ray, who was a member of this class, states: "We had one small textbook, the one teacher and once a week recitations, but the instruction covered or (to speak more accurately) touched upon nearly everything taught in seminary today."⁶

Carroll's assistance to young ministers was not limited to the classroom setting. During his ministry First Baptist, Waco, ordained many ministerial students and Carroll "laid himself out to make every ordination great." P. E. Burroughs, one such student, had just graduated from the university, when a church requested that First Baptist ordain Burroughs so that he might become their pastor.

Carroll sent for Burroughs to come to his home; and upon Burroughs' arrival Carroll took him into the library, showed him a selection of books, and stated: "Devour these books; I am near you; refer any questions to me." Burroughs was ordained a week later. He would say in reference to his ordination that as the years went by he could still feel the pressure of Carroll's hands upon his head and hear Carroll saying: "God bless you and make you a good minister of Jesus Christ."[7]

The merger of the two state conventions in 1886 brought additional responsibilities to Carroll in the area of education. Baylor University, at Independence, and Waco University were consolidated into Baylor University at Waco; and the new board of trustees elected Carroll as their president, a position he would hold until 1907.[8] Immediately the financial situation of this consolidated school became one of Carroll's chief concerns. After years of urging by Carroll, in 1891 Baylor hired George W. Truett as a financial agent to help reduce the university's debt. First Baptist, Waco, gave Carroll a leave from his pulpit from June to October of 1891 to assist Truett in a fundraising endeavor.[9]

Despite increased demands upon his time due to his involvement with the administration of Baylor, Carroll continued to be an effective teacher, and his classes for ministerial students grew throughout the 1880s. His training of these students was so well known by 1890 that talk originated of his class becoming the foundation for a theological department at the university. Carroll responded by saying:

> We have never claimed to have a theological department, nor do we issue diplomas to that effect. But we do furnish facilities for great improvement in this direction by way of preparation for a regular theological seminary. Regular lectures are delivered and courses of reading and study marked out to those young ministers.[10]

The continued growth of this ministerial training soon demanded that a formal structure for it be created within the curriculum of the university. Therefore, in 1893, with an enrollment of seventy-five students, Baylor University established a Bible Department and named Carroll to the chair of Exegesis and Systematic Theology, Burleson to the chair of Pastoral Duties, and J. H. Luther to the chair of Homiletics.[11] After the loss of Luther, Baylor reorganized the department in 1894, at which time the enrollment totaled only forty students. The university did not give Carroll an official

John Tanner
— Courtesy Southwestern Baptist Theological Seminary Archives

title under the reorganization but listed him as directing studies of the Bible in the classroom and listed Burleson as regularly lecturing on "Church History, Homiletics, and kindred subjects."[12] The 1895 report on ministerial education indicated that the Bible Department's enrollment figure had increased; that W. A. Harris, professor of Greek at Baylor, had joined the department to teach New Testament; and that Carroll now had the title of "principal of the Bible Department."[13]

In 1896 Baylor added John S. Tanner to the growing faculty of the Bible Department. Tanner, who graduated from Baylor with a B.A. degree in 1890, taught classes at Baylor while working on his M.A. degree, which was awarded in 1893. Upon his graduation from Southern Baptist Theological Seminary in 1895, Tanner wrote to Carroll seeking advice on whether he should begin work on a Ph.D. at the University of Chicago. He also made no secret of his desire to return to Baylor:

> I wanted to ask you about the present outlook for Baylor University and the developments of the past few years. While there is no commitment on either side, yet I have all along entertained the feeling that my work is in Texas in connection with Baylor. Your views on this subject, as freely given as you feel justified, would be appreciated. I can modestly say that it is not a question of getting a job, but of spending my life where God can use it to most effect.[14]

After completing his studies at the University of Chicago, Tanner returned to Baylor in 1897 and quickly organized the first Summer Bible School at the university. The school grew rapidly and by 1898 had an enrollment of 252 students.[15] Baker credited Tanner as being, next to Carroll, "the most influential individual in laying the groundwork for the new seminary in the Southwest."[16] W. T. Conner called him "the most inspiring teacher I ever knew."[17] History can only speculate the impact that Tanner would have had on the early days of the new Texas seminary; for on March 21, 1901, J. S. Tanner died.

THE WHITSITT CONTROVERSY

Southern Baptist Theological Seminary elected William Heth Whitsitt to the faculty in 1872 and named him president of the school in 1895 after the death of John A. Broadus. W. O. Carver states that "no man in the history of the Southern Baptist Theological Seminary ever received so little recognition for so great a service as William Heth Whitsitt."[18]

As a professor of church history Whitsitt had a keen interest in one of the most pressing issues of his day — Baptist church succession. In the summer of 1880 Whitsitt traveled to Great Britain to study this issue in the libraries of Oxford and Cambridge as well as to examine manuscripts in the British Museum. After three months of research, Whitsitt concluded that prior to 1641 English Baptists had used sprinkling and pouring as methods of baptism rather than immersion, as was widely believed. From this conclusion Whitsitt reasoned that Roger Williams, the founder of the first Baptist Church in America, had been sprinkled at baptism rather than immersed.[19]

Upon his return to the United States, Whitsitt published the results of his research in two unsigned editorials in the September issues of a New York-based, non-denominational paper known as the *Independent*. Aware of the controversy that his findings might inaugurate, Whitsitt published the editorials anonymously so that criticism of his findings would not be directed at him or the seminary.[20] In 1895, fifteen years after the original publication of his research, Whitsitt wrote the article that would spark the controversy that bears his name. The article on Baptists appeared in *Johnson's Universal Cyclopaedia*, and unlike the 1880 editorials this work was signed. Immediately upon release of the article Whitsitt's concerns, which had forced him to publish anonymously in 1880, were realized. People who followed the Landmark teachings of J. R. Graves began to vocally criticize Whitsitt and the seminary.

Whitsitt's conclusions drew ire because they called into question the unbroken existence of Baptist churches from the New Testament era until modern times. This belief, known as Baptist church succession, was one of the major teachings of Landmarkism. Although the Southern Baptist Convention never officially endorsed the Landmark teachings of J. R. Graves, many local Baptist churches, particularly in the Southwest, did accept Landmarkism. Although attempts by Landmarkists to control the Southern Baptist Convention during the late 1800s had failed on numerous occasions, many perceived the threat to be a real possibility. In the only known correspondence between Whitsitt and Carroll, Whitsitt shared his concern about the upcoming convention in 1895: "Have you any reason to suspect that an assault is being planned against the Southern Baptist Convention, whether from our side of the river, or your side, or both sides."[21] In order to defend Baptist church succession, many Baptists believed that they had to defeat W. H. Whitsitt. Caught in the middle of this battle was the board of trustees of Southern Baptist Theological Seminary, of which B. H. Carroll was a member.

EARLY ROLE

From the outset of the Whitsitt Controversy, men on both sides of the issue realized the importance of B. H. Carroll's opinion and the influence that it could have on the entire convention. In his initial statement on the controversy, entitled "Dr. Carroll Has a Word About the Whitsitt Controversy," Carroll expressed moderate opinions on the issue. He stated that the controversy did not concern doctrinal issues but concerned "human history." Carroll also believed that Whitsitt was not denying Baptist principles with his conclusions, that indeed these principles to which Whitsitt adhered could be traced to the first century even if "Baptist Churches" could not be.[22]

The Southern Baptist Convention's annual meeting of May 1896, in Chattanooga, was the first national gathering of Baptists since the controversy had erupted. The convention did not adopt an official statement on the controversy, but the messengers did request that the seminary trustees report on the powers that the convention had over Southern. Carroll, in reporting for the trustees, stated that the convention had no legal authority to appoint or to remove members of the faculty or board of trustees. He also added that while the board had a moral obligation to reflect the beliefs of the convention as well as to seek its advice, the seminary could also operate independently of the convention.[23]

Carroll tried to remain a voice of moderation in the early stages of the controversy, however, pressure mounted from both sides for him to take a stand. On June 12, 1896, in the earliest existing correspondence sent to Carroll about the controversy. A. B. Miller of Bonham, Texas, sought Carroll's opinion on Whitsitt and then volunteered his own, stating:

> For my part I do not think such a man should be retained as a member of a Baptist church, much less as a professor or president of a Baptist Theological Seminary.[24]

Carroll apparently responded quickly to Miller's first letter; for a second letter from Miller dated July 3, 1896, thanks Carroll for unknown "valuable information." In this letter Miller appears confident that "something shall be done to remove the present distressing embarrassment."[25] During the early stages of the controversy, Carroll no doubt received other letters critical of Whitsitt, although none remains. Fortunately, the Miller letters provide ample insight into the early anti-Whitsitt movement.

Pro-Whitsitt forces realized the importance of Carroll's support as well. A. T. Robertson, a faculty member at Southern during the controversy and perhaps the greatest scholar in the history of Southern Baptists, wrote to Carroll in July 1896, stating that Whitsitt had a "very strong case that ought to be given a candid hearing." Robertson went on to state his frustration over the treatment that Whitsitt was receiving from fellow Baptists:

> I am sick and tired of all this fuss and feathers, tempest in a teapot. Dr. Whitsitt is a gentleman, a Christian, and a Baptist and merits courteous treatment. Is there anything you can do to help quiet all this furor?[26]

Perhaps the most prophetic letter concerning Carroll's role in the unfolding controversy came from John R. Sampey, also on faculty at Southern. Sampey wrote to Carroll to inform him that Whitsitt's book *A Question in Baptist History*, which explained his conclusions in detail, would be published by September. He continued:

> It occurs to me to say to you that the eyes of many thousands of our people will be fastened on you pretty soon after the appearance of this little book, and they will look with interest to see what you think of the argument. Don't forget the responsibility resting on you to speak the truth in love. Your opinion will be final with thousands of people who are not in the habit of doing their own thinking, while at the same time powerfully influencing the most thoughtful of our brethern *[sic]*. I trust the Lord will give you the right word to speak.[27]

As anti-Whitsitt sentiment increased throughout Texas during 1896, Carroll continued to retain his moderate stand. During the annual meeting of the Baptist General Convention of Texas, Carroll was able to use his influence to push through a moderate resolution on the Whitsitt issue. In part it said:

> Resolved, That we respectfully and lovingly, but very earnestly,

refer this whole matter to the trustees of the Seminary having jur-
isdiction over the case, as worthy of their most serious consideration, and do earnestly request from them, assembled in annual session at Wilmington, NC, next May, a clear-cut deliverance on the
merits of the whole case, according to all the merits of the whole
case, according to all the facts. And that this deliverance be submitted to the Southern Baptist Convention, then and there in session, for such action as may be lawful and right.[28]

Carroll could make no promises concerning the trustees' actions, but he did assure his fellow Texas Baptists that he would carry
their concerns with him to Wilmington and that the board would act.

MEETING AT WILMINGTON

The board of trustees met at 10:00 A.M. on May 6, 1897, just
prior to the Southern Baptist Convention's annual meeting. After
various memorials were presented to the trustees, Carroll offered a
resolution designed to address the concerns mentioned in the Texas
Resolution of October 1896. Carroll's resolution called for the
board to examine Whitsitt's writings, to "pronounce upon them
clearly according to our best judgment of the facts and merits of the
case," and to report the findings to the convention.[29] However, W. J.
Northen, a trustee from Georgia, introduced a substitute motion
that stated:

> The Trustees of the Southern Baptist Theological Seminary,
> assembled in their annual meeting in Wilmington, N.C. May 6,
> 1897, desire to submit to the Baptists of the South the following
> statement in regard to the institution whose interests have been
> committed to their care and management.
>   1) That we account this a fitting occasion to reaffirm our cor-
> dial and thorough adherence to the Fundamental Articles adopted
> at a time when the seminary was established and to assure those in
> whose behalf we hold in trust and administer the affairs of this
> institution that it is our steadfast purpose to require in the future
> as in the past that the Fundamental Laws and scriptural doctrines
> embodied in these articles shall be faithfully upheld by those who
> occupy chairs as teachers.
>   2) That we cannot undertake to sit in judgment upon ques-
> tions of Baptist history which do not imperil any of these prin-
> ciples concerning which all Baptists are agreed, but concerning
> which serious, conscientious, and scholarly students are not agreed.

We can, however, leave to continued research and free discussion the satisfactory solution of these.

3) That, believing the Seminary to hold an important (position) relative to the prosperity and usefulness of Southern Baptists, we consider it our duty, while demanding of those in charge of its department of instruction, the utmost patience in research and the greatest discretion in utterance, to foster, rather than repress the spirit of earnest and reverent investigation.

4) That, having fully assured that the tender affection which we cherish for this institution founded by our fathers and bequeathed by them to us, is shared by the Baptists of the South, we can safely trust them, as we ask them to trust us, to guard its honor, promote its usefulness, and pray for its prosperity.[30]

Each motion was debated, and finally the substitute motion presented by Northen was approved. Carroll stated that one reason this motion won approval was that:

we tentatively adopt[ed] the substitute — not as a finality, but to allow Dr. Whitsitt to make any statements he might be able to make conscientiously, without embarrassment. It was hoped by many that his statement might so relieve the situation as to permit the adoption of the substitute as a finality.[31]

The board appointed Carroll, along with W. E. Hatcher and H. McDonald, to invite Whitsitt to make a statement before the trustees. This statement and resolution were presented to the convention later as a matter of information with no action to be taken.

In the eyes of many Whitsitt supporters, the controversy was finally over. Upon his return from Wilmington, Whitsitt issued a call for peace in an address to the students at the seminary:

Let us all be considerate of our beloved brethren, sincere and devoted men. Though we differ with them and they from us, we have faith in them. Let us cultivate that faith more and more. Let us esteem and honor them. Let us love them honestly and heartily. They are strong and worthy men. I believe that none of them will reject the olive branch that we offer. On the contrary, they will be glad of any sincere and kindly advance that we may make. Let nothing be said or done to give them pain. They are not striving to lord it over us; neither do we desire to lord it over them. They are honored brethren; in God's name let us love them as Christian brethren.

. . . I request that everyone will earnestly pray for the peace of

Jesus. We are weary of strife and bitterness. We sincerely desire the respect and sympathy of all our brethren. Peace will promote the glory of God and the comfort of souls. Peace will cheer our aching hearts. O Lord, send peace, sweet peace, holy peace, for thy name's sake. . . . Peace will introduce a season of great work. Holy Ghost religion and hard work are the best things in the world for Baptists.[32]

ROLE AFTER WILMINGTON

If Whitsitt returned to Southern as the victorious warrior calling for peace, Carroll returned to Texas as the defeated knight desiring a rematch. The decision of the Board at Wilmington damaged Carroll's image not only in Texas but throughout the Southwest. Keith Cogburn states that Carroll felt betrayed by the board's actions at Wilmington. Upon hearing the initial press reports of the meeting, Baptists in the Southwest, however, felt betrayed by Carroll. Carroll had promised action on the Whitsitt matter, yet none was taken. Area Baptists throughout the Southwest wanted an explanation of what had occurred at the meeting from Carroll's perspective. In response Carroll wrote "The Whitsitt Case at Wilmington," which appeared in the *Baptist Standard* on May 20, 1897.

"The Whitsitt Case" was the first of several articles that Carroll wrote during 1897 on the Whitsitt affair. At this time Carroll shifted to assume a strong anti-Whitsitt position due to one small phrase in the Northen motion — "we cannot undertake to sit in judgment." The correspondence that Carroll received after publication of the Whitsitt articles indicates his continued influence among Southern Baptists.

In "Back to the Realm of Discussion," Carroll addressed the regional aspect of the controversy with reference to his conversations with the common people of the western section of the convention "mainly in Kentucky, Mississippi, Louisiana, Arkansas and Texas, where J. R. Graves' 'soul goes marching on.'"[33] These were the people whom Carroll felt were ignored by the settlement at Wilmington; their concerns were forgotten with the phrase "we cannot undertake to sit in judgment."

For B. H. Carroll, Whitsitt and his conclusions on Baptists' recovery of the practice of immersion became a secondary issue. On August 5, 1897, Carroll published an article in the *Baptist Standard* entitled "The Real Issue in the Whitsitt Case":

As I expect to stand before the judgment bar and answer to my Lord for my conduct and stewardship on earth, I do solemnly aver and avow that the main question in this case is not Eaton vs. Whitsitt, is not a mere question of English Baptist history, is not 'shall Landmarkism be arbitrarily forced on the Seminary for dogmatic teaching,' is not this or that theory of organic church succession, is not traditionalism versus the Scriptures.[34]

The real issue, according to Carroll, was the unity of the convention. He saw "extremists" from both sides of the controversy "hammering wedges" in an attempt to divide the convention regionally. Carroll believed that it would be better for the seminary to perish than for a split to occur. He stated: "We may be able to establish another seminary, we can never put together again the fragments of this great convention if once the unity is broken."[35]

In what some see as an effort to protect this unity, Carroll introduced the following motion at the 1898 convention to provide information only, not to be voted on:

Resolved, That this Convention, without expressing any opinion whatever on the merits of the controversy concerning Seminary matters, about which good brethren among us honestly differ, but in the interest of harmony, particularly with a view to preserve and confirm unity in mission work, does now exercise its evident right to divest itself of responsibility in the Seminary management, by dissolving the slight and remote bond of connection between this body and the Seminary; that is, that this body declines to nominate trustees for the Seminary or to entertain motions or receive reports relative thereto, leaving the Institution to stand on its own merits and be managed by its own trustees.[36]

Carroll announced that he would bring the motion to the floor for consideration at the convention in 1899. Carroll had at last forced the hands of Whitsitt supporters. To avoid severing convention ties to the seminary, Whitsitt would have to be removed. A. T. Robertson, one of Whitsitt's strongest supporters, wrote to J. R. Sampey on July 10, 1898, stating: "I have written Whitsitt giving him ten reasons why he ought to announce his resignation just before the Missouri Convention."[37] Three days later Whitsitt tendered his resignation effective at the end of the 1898–99 academic year.

The board of trustees unanimously elected Dr. E. Y. Mullins on June 29, 1899, to be president of Southern Seminary. James Tull notes that the choice of Mullins was interesting as he was a Whitsitt supporter and had no Landmark ties. In addition W. J. McGlothlin, who replaced Whitsitt as professor of church history, ironically agreed with Whitsitt's conclusions concerning Baptist history.[38]

The *American Baptist Flag* nominated Carroll to replace Whitsitt as president of Southern Seminary. In an editorial dated October 6, 1898, G. A. Coulson opposed this nomination saying that although Carroll was a personal friend, a splendid preacher, "and well up on history" he opposed the nomination because:

> 1. He is ambitious, and that spirit predominates to such an extent that his judgment is warped, and he will stoop to things that are wrong to carry his point. . . . 2. He prosecuted a preacher for heresy, a member of his own church, and before his own church, without a legal council. Had the church to take away the credentials of the preacher and then give him a letter of full fellowship. All these things he advocated before the church, or to say the least, acquiesced in them. Dr. Carroll is not sound on Bible repentance. He never uttered a word against the position of Whitsitt till he saw how the people were going. But these are enough. I am one among the thousands in Texas who do not want B. H. Carroll, of Waco, to supercede W. H. Whitsitt as president.

There is no record of the board's ever having considered Carroll to replace Whitsitt as president.[39]

SUMMARY

In examining Carroll's role in the Whitsitt affair, three distinct facts emerge. First, the actions of the board at Wilmington forced Carroll to shift from his moderate position to an anti-Whitsitt position. He had put his reputation on the line with many Texas Baptists in 1896 by pushing for a moderate Whitsitt resolution that called upon the trustees to act on the matter. No doubt many thought that Carroll's position on the board would ensure that this action would be taken. Carroll's resolution called for neither a condemnation nor affirmation of Whitsitt but for a clear pronouncement from the Board concerning "the facts and merits of the case." By refusing to "sit in judgment," the board indicated that the concerns of Texas and the Southwest were not important. One can only speculate what the final result of the bontroversy might have been had Carroll's resolution passed.

The second fact to emerge from the Whitsitt affair was that Carroll's resolution to sever ties with the seminary was not in the interest of preserving the convention but rather to force the pro-Whitsitt forces to act. The pro-Whitsitt forces, in response, acted to preserve the union of the convention. In a confidential letter to Carroll, F. H. Kerfoot used the illustration of Abraham Lincoln and Alexander Stephens at the Monroe Conference to show the feelings that the pro-Whitsitt forces had toward the controversy. Kerfoot recalled how Lincoln wrote "Union" in large letters on a piece of paper, handed it to Stephens, and said: "Write whatever you please and I'll agree to it."[40] If Whitsitt supporters had handed Carroll a paper with "Unity" written on it, he would have written "remove Whitsitt." Without a doubt the convention was important to Carroll; had the controversy continued one wonders if Carroll would have compromised to save the convention or allowed the split to occur and then assumed leadership of a Southwestern Baptist Convention.

The final fact to emerge from the Whitsitt affair was the real issue of the Whitsitt Controversy as far as Carroll was concerned. Carroll addressed the controversy in general terms by examining the unity of the convention, but he never publicly addressed the issue in its simplest form, that of a question: Is the Southern Baptist Theological Seminary truly the seminary of the entire convention? Although Carroll did not answer the question during the controversy, he answered it through his actions a few years later when he became the driving force behind the founding of Southwestern Baptist Theological Seminary.

If Whitsitt's conclusions regarding baptism were the major issues in the controversy, then as W. W. Barnes says, Carroll's group "won the battle, but lost the war."[41] Southern Seminary continued to support and to teach Whitsitt's views, as seen with the appointment of Mullins and McGlothin to the faculty. Carroll, in a letter to the *Baptist Courier* on March 18, 1898, called for a balance at the seminary in presenting the Landmark and anti-Landmark element in Baptist history. This call for balance was apparently never addressed, and the controversy ended with Whitsitt's resignation. Although anti-Whitsitt supporters won the controversy, Whitsitt's conclusions were both accepted and taught by many Baptist church historians, including those at the seminary that Carroll would establish in Texas. This irony did not escape A. T. Robertson, who in an address in the *Baptist World* in 1911 stated: "All our seminaries, including the one in Texas, now teach what Whitsitt claimed." Robertson later wrote to Carroll to explain that his statement was not intended to imply that Carroll, himself, now supported Whitsitt but that those teaching church history at Southwestern did.[42]

FOUNDING OF SOUTHWESTERN
BAPTIST THEOLOGICAL SEMINARY

During the Baptist General Convention of 1898, R. C. Buckner read a three-word telegram explaining the absence of B. H. Carroll. This telegram, which also helped to explain upcoming changes in Carroll's life, read: "Wife is dying."[43] After her death Carroll described himself as a lonely man. At this time Carroll's brother J. M. began trying to persuade Carroll to give his final years to the improvement of ministerial education. But convincing Carroll to leave First Baptist was no easy task:

> He was devoted to his church and the church was devoted to him.
> They had been together some 28 years. These ties would have to
> be broken. It was a trying situation, but B. H. Carroll was finally
> tremendously impressed with this school movement.[44]

Carroll initially resisted his brother's plea, but with his resignation from First Baptist Church, Waco, in January 1899, he joined J. M.'s work.

Carroll's full-time work with the Education Commission lasted only a short time, possibly explaining its omission by Jeff D. Ray, J. W. Crowder, J. B. Cranfill, and Frank Burkhalter in their accounts of Carroll's life. In addition, although Carroll resigned the pastorate at First Baptist, Waco, there is no record of his resigning his position at Baylor, which may also explain why these men saw Carroll's resignation from First Baptist as a move toward full-time work with Baylor.

Baker makes an interesting statement about Carroll's move from the pastorate to the Education Commission:

> It cannot be known whether he [Carroll] went a step further in his
> thinking and envisioned the enlarged program at Baylor as an op-
> portunity for him to engage directly in that program. It seems
> quite certain that he did not have in mind organizing a theological
> seminary at this time.[45]

In his resignation Carroll stated:

In the general cause of Christian education is involved the work of

B. H. Carroll about 1900.
— Courtesy Southwestern Baptist Theological Seminary Archives

Hallie Harrison Carroll, B. H. Carroll's third wife, married Carroll in 1899.
— Courtesy Southwestern Baptist Theological Seminary Archives

the Bible Department of Baylor University, which more than any other agency possesses the solution of the thousand ills which have heretofore afflicted and crippled us.[46]

The use of the phrase "possesses the solution" may indicate that Carroll did envision the enlargement of the Bible Department at Baylor which would lead to a theological seminary. "The thousand ills which have heretofore afflicted and crippled us" may refer to the regional tensions between the East and the Southwest which arose, in part, because of the Whitsitt Controversy. Using this interpretation, the solution that Baylor "possessed" might have been education for ministerial students of the Southwest in the Southwest. There is also evidence in Carroll's correspondence concerning the Whitsitt affair that the founding of a new seminary by Carroll was a possible solution to the controversy. In a letter from R. B. Morgan to B. H. Carroll dated May 2, 1897, Morgan sounded almost prophetic as he offered Carroll his solution to the controversy. He stated:

> Do you not think it is time for the South and West to have a Theological institution to train her young preachers, under the control of, and manned by Baptists. Is not Baylor the location and is not this the time. You have already made the start of a Bible department. Why not let it assume the proportions of a Seminary proper? . . . Texas needs just such a place today.[47]

There is no record of Carroll openly suggesting a new seminary as a solution at this time, but he must have considered the possibility. Both Carroll's resignation and his correspondence seem to indicate that he did realize that the department might evolve into a seminary.

THE THEOLOGICAL DEPARTMENT AT BAYLOR

In 1900 Carroll's title as principal of the Bible Department was changed to dean of the Bible Department.[48] Though subtle, the change was a foreshadowing of events to come. In 1901 Carroll, with the full support of the president of Baylor, announced the creation of the Theological Department of Baylor. Baylor named Carroll as dean. Although his title had changed, he continued to collect no salary. Soon many Texas Baptists began to contribute to the endowment of this new Theological Department.[49]

Two new professors were added to the department's faculty during its first year — A. H. Newman and R. N. Barrett. Newman was a well-recognized church historian who helped to bring instant credibility to the new department. Barrett, pastor of First Baptist, Waxahachie, and a close friend of John Tanner, was hired to teach biblical language and missions. One of Carroll's greatest abilities during these formative years was in persuading well-recognized and highly qualified instructors to come to Baylor and to be a part of this new endeavor.[50] If Tanner had not suffered an untimely death, the scholarship of the new Theological Department at Baylor might have rivaled the existing scholarship at Southern Seminary.

Carroll resigned his position with the Education Commission in 1902 to devote himself fully to the new Theological Department. He did not receive a salary, however, until January 1904.[51] The financial needs of the department grew from 1901 to 1905, causing Carroll to ask the board of trustees for permission to raise money for the department during the summer of 1905 in order to enlarge the curriculum and to hire additional faculty. Carroll's plan was to raise funds to support the department for three years (1905–08). The funds raised would pay the salaries of all teachers employed by the Theological Department, thus enabling the university to save thousands of dollars a year on teachers' salaries. The funds would also allow Carroll to hire additional faculty providing that the trustees approved and that money was available in the department's funds. The trustees granted Carroll's request. As a result of this campaign, Calvin Goodspeed and C. B. Williams were added to the faculty.[52]

S. P. Brooks, president of Baylor since 1902, issued a report to the Baptist General Convention of Texas in 1905 noting the approval by the board of the fundraising campaign for the Theological Department as well as the addition of the new faculty. Brooks omitted mentioning another resolution, which was passed at the same meeting, concerning the Theological Department. The resolution stated

> that Baylor University now make the Theological Department a complete School of Divinity — teaching all the courses and conferring all the degrees of a regular first class theological seminary, provided that no debt on the university is contracted in prosecuting this work. . . .[53]

DENIALS CONCERNING NEW BAPTIST SEMINARY

Baylor had long been uncomfortable with defining its role in the theological education of young ministers. As noted, Carroll issued a denial that Baylor was starting a Department of Theology in 1890. By 1893, however, Baylor would have a Bible Department which in 1901 would become a Theological Department. From 1901 to 1905 many people connected with Baylor, including Carroll, continued to deny that Baylor was starting a seminary.

The creation of a seminary in Texas seemed a natural step to many Southern Baptists in 1901, including some Baptists on the East Coast. J. W. Bailey, editor of North Carolina's *Biblical Recorder*, stated in an editorial on July 10, 1901:

> with such a host of Baptists as Texas counts, it is not unreasonable that it be made the home of a theological school which shall hold the young men thus educated to their own section of the country.[54]

R. N. Barrett, a faculty member of the new department at Baylor, fueled speculation that the department would become a seminary by stating that after sufficient funds were raised, the Theological Department would proceed "with the full curriculum of a well-organized seminary."[55]

Opposition to the enlargement of the Theological Department into a seminary would soon be encountered from a most unexpected source — the new president of Baylor, S. P. Brooks. The position that Brooks found himself in as president of the university is best described by Baker:

> He was not pleased with the unique administrative structure which had existed for several years at the Waco school. B. H. Carroll was regularly elected as president of the board of trustees and in this capacity exercised a considerable amount of authority over the president of the school. This situation was not critical during the time Carroll was pastor of the Waco church, but when he came to the faculty of Baylor to teach Bible, it produced a remarkable administrative structure in which the president of the university found himself under the authority of one of his faculty. Conscious of this paradox, Brooks moved to assert the prerogatives of his position. No longer did Carroll report to the state convention as chairman of the trustees, but from the time Brooks came in 1902 it was he who made these reports as president. He, like R. C. Burleson, believed that a preacher needed first of all a

strong literary education like any other student, after which the distinctive ministerial training could be added. He kept a careful watch on the new department.[56]

In Brooks' 1903 report before the Baptist General Convention of Texas, he emphasized:

[the] Theological School at Baylor University in no sense is, or expects to be a rival to our own seminary at Louisville. . . . So long as the Seminary can offer, as it clearly does now, more Theological training than Baylor, we shall continue to encourage our students to go there for the so-called completion of their studies.[57]

J. W. Bailey, who had two years earlier said that he did not think that it was "unreasonable" for Texas to start a theological school, stated in 1903 that Baylor was attempting to do so. On March 12, Bailey wrote that "Baylor has been bidding for a place as rival of the Louisville Seminary with the Whitsitt Controversy as a basis."[58] This statement brought a quick and somewhat heated response from Carroll, who stated that Baylor's department had no desire to be the seminary rival and that the Whitsitt Controversy had nothing to do with developments occurring at Baylor.[59] While one could agree, along with Carroll, that the Theological Department at Baylor was not attempting to rival Southern but was simply meeting the ministerial training needs of the Southwest, one could not agree with Carroll's statement concerning the role of the Whitsitt Controversy. Although the Whitsitt Controversy was not the only basis for starting a seminary in Texas, as Bailey advocated in his 1901 editorial, the controversy did play an important role in showing Carroll and others in the Southwest that Southern was not the seminary of the entire convention.

BAYLOR THEOLOGICAL SEMINARY

When Carroll presented his resolution on August 31, 1905, calling for Baylor to make the Theological Department a seminary, S. P. Brooks was in Europe. At that meeting Carroll shared with the board a "vision" he had that summer while traveling to Amarillo by train. In the vision God showed Carroll the need for a theological school to educate ministers in the Southwest. When Carroll heard a voice say: "Whom will I send and who will go for us?," he answered: "Lord, it is clearly thy will; what is impossible with man is possible with God; go thou with me and I will try." When the vision was over, Carroll found himself standing and gripping the back of the seat in front of him. Many of the passengers were looking at him with "amusement" and "amazement." Carroll stated that he sat down, feeling "confused, embarrassed and humiliated."[60] This vision is often seen as Carroll's "sign from God" to establish the seminary, yet the Theological Department was well on its way to becoming a seminary at that time. Therefore the vision should be seen as an affirmation of the direction in which Carroll was going rather than as a call for him to begin the seminary.

In the emotion of the moment following Carroll's presentation, the trustees approved the resolution without consulting the university's president. In fact, not until Brooks returned did he learn that one of his departments had become a separate institution.[61] This situation might also explain why Brooks failed to report the resolution in his 1905 address to the Baptist General Convention of Texas, for he could not explain to the convention the impact of the decision when he did not fully understand it himself.

In his opening address to the Theological Department, printed in the *Baptist Standard* on September 14, 1905, Carroll listed five reasons that described the necessity of establishing a seminary in Texas: 1) no seminary existed in the Southwest, 2) many preachers who attended Southern remained in that part of the country, 3) preachers "loose in doctrine" were invading the Southwest, 4) many of the Southwest's preachers were uneducated, 5) the West was rapidly developing. Carroll also addressed what he called the "negative intent of this movement." With the words of Bailey's 1903 editorial ringing in his ears, Carroll stated:

> This proposed enlargement of our work is not in opposition to rivalry or supersession of our Southern Baptist Theological Seminary, with which we desire the most friendly relations, which desire doubtless they will reciprocate, but is based upon our deep conviction that no one seminary can train all the preachers of the South and the Southwest. It is needed work here to which we address ourselves — work dear alike to them and to us.
>
> It is evident, also, from the school roll of Northern seminaries that they are not supplying the need in this great Southwestern section. Moreover, this move on our part is not intended to discourage or depreciate the valuable work done in most Baptist literary schools in partial ministerial training. When all is done, that all of us are doing, we will fall short of meeting the necessities of the case.[62]

Baker notes that Bailey did not delay in replying to Carroll's address. In a September 27 editorial Bailey stated: "Once upon a time we pointed out that another theological seminary was raising in Baylor University, Texas; and promptly did we receive most weighty denials from the men in charge." Carroll never replied.[63]

Baker also states that the seminary in Louisville was "gracious in its general response to the development of a new Baptist seminary in Texas." Apparently, John A. Broadus had predicted the possibility of a new seminary to John R. Sampey years before. In a July 14, 1943, letter to W. W. Barnes, professor of church history at Southwestern Baptist Theological Seminary, Sampey stated:

> During the closing years of the life of Doctor Broadus, especially after the death of Doctor Basil Manly in January, 1892, he frequently invited me to join him in his afternoon walks. On one of these he said to me, "It will not be long before another theological seminary will be founded among Southern Baptists, and it will probably be in Texas." He then added to his young colleague one significant remark, "When the new seminary comes, it ought to be with the good will of the Southern Seminary."[64]

Carroll made the first report of the Baylor Theological Seminary at the Baptist General Convention of Texas' annual meeting in 1906. In his report Carroll noted that as dean of the seminary he had taken on the responsibility of raising funds for the seminary as well as for teaching "very large classes" in Old and New Testament English Bible for ten months a year. Carroll also called for the first chair of the seminary to be endowed, stating that it should be the chair of Evangelism.[65]

In reviewing the seminary's first year, Carroll noted that 140 preachers were enrolled in addition to many laymen and women preparing for denominational service. He continued:

> No other Seminary on the Western Continent ever had so large and prosperous a beginning. Five regular professors, two special teachers, and many special lecturers have been employed. Every department of theological work has been well taught. No other Seminary has a higher grade of theological study and in some respects our curriculum requirements are higher than any other. No other Seminary provides a four year's course in the English Bible.[66]

Although the seminary received high praise from many Texas

Baptist leaders in 1906, Carroll arrived at the Baptist General Convention of Texas' annual meeting in 1907 still fighting for the seminary's right to exist.[67] An article which appeared in the *Baptist Standard* the week of the convention appealed to the messengers to help raise the endowment of Southern. Carroll did not object to this plea; however, the second paragraph contained what he called "a fly in the apothecary's ointment." The paragraph made the following three statements: 1) Southern Baptists have but one theological seminary, 2) Southern Baptists desire but one theological seminary, 3) Southern Baptists are agreed to have just one theological seminary. Carroll addressed each one of these statements and defended Baylor Theological Seminary's right to exist in his report to the convention. As part of his defense, Carroll cited the inaugural address of James P. Boyce:

> The object is not centralization of power in a single institution for I believe that the adoption of these changes will make many seminaries necessary. I advocate a single [seminary] now because the demand for more than one does not exist.[68]

At the time of Carroll's report many Southern Baptists, both in Texas and throughout the convention, were skeptical of this new seminary and of the impact that it would have on ministerial education.

BREAK WITH BAYLOR

As the seminary began to establish itself among Texas Baptists, it began to cause tension at the institution which had given it birth. The first mention of this tension came at the Baylor Board of Trustees meeting on October 15, 1906. The trustees appointed a committee to study the friction between the Literary and Theological departments and to report back to the board its findings and recommendations.[69]

Although the committee would not make its recommendations for some time, Carroll announced his solutions in a report that he prepared for the board in the spring of 1907. Carroll stated: "A Theological Seminary . . . must ultimately be placed on its own distinct habitat and under a distinct charter and management."[70] Carroll stated that it was "premature" to consider a separation now; however, he believed that the board should follow a course in this direction. S. P. Brooks, who was not at the meeting, quickly responded to

Baylor Theological Seminary in 1907, one year before becoming Southwestern Seminary. George W. Truett is seated front row center next to B. H. Carroll.
— Courtesy Southwestern Baptist Theological Seminary Archives

Samuel P. Brooks, president of Baylor University.
— Courtesy Southwestern Baptist Theological Seminary Archives

Carroll's statement in a personal letter dated June 26, 1907, in which Brooks stated: "I regret to dissent from the conclusions reached in that communication."[71]

Brooks' opposition to the call for separation was not surprising, as he had felt uncomfortable with the creation of the Theological Department from the beginning. Had he been at the original meeting, he doubtlessly would have spoken against the creation of the seminary. There is no evidence that Brooks was opposed to founding a new seminary in Texas; he objected to the dangerous precedent that was being set for other departments within the university. For example, the Business Department could announce that it wanted to separate from the university as well, using the Theological Department's actions as a model. For whatever reasons that Brooks opposed separation, his opposition was short-lived.

On September 19, 1907, three days after the board failed to come to an agreement on a report concerning the relationship between the Theological and Literary departments, Brooks wrote to Carroll announcing his support for separation. In his letter Brooks clearly stated that the separation should be absolute. Jeff D. Ray had recommended that the institution be separate from the university but remain located at Baylor. Brooks disagreed, stating: "I do not believe it should separate and remain in Baylor or in Waco."[72]

The reason behind Brooks' "so complete a reversal of judgments" is unknown. Perhaps counsel received from other Baptist leaders influenced him.[73] Perhaps an unrecorded meeting between Carroll and Brooks occurred in which Carroll promised to resign from the Baylor Board of Trustees if a separation were achieved. Although the latter is pure speculation, such an agreement no doubt would have appealed to Brooks. Whatever the reason, Carroll and Brooks were now in agreement.

At the board meeting on September 30, 1907, the trustees passed the following recommendation that would be presented to the Baptist General Convention of Texas at its annual meeting in November:

> Your committee appointed to suggest a plan to harmonize differences between the literary and theological departments of the University, report as follows:
>
> 1st. — We recommend that the Board of Trustees request the convention to immediately incorporate the Seminary with its domicile at Waco until, if ever, it seemed most to the interest of the Redeemer's Kingdom to remove it elsewhere.

2nd. — That till its charter is obtained the Seminary be conducted under the same plan and arrangements as now in operation.

3rd. — That the charter name of the Seminary shall be such as to clearly differentiate it from Baylor University at Waco, Texas.

4th. — That in case our request is granted by the convention, the University will continue to furnish teaching quarters to the Seminary, temporarily, till suitable accommodations can be provided for it.[74]

After Ray made these recommendations to the convention, an appointed committee of fifteen studied them and two days later reported to the convention that it should "grant the request of the board of trustees of Baylor." The committee also stated that though the seminary was leaving Baylor, Baylor should continue to train ministers, including instruction in "English Bible" if the leadership at Baylor thought it to be "proper" and "justified." The report was unanimously adopted.[75] Baylor and its seminary were now separate institutions.

Carroll's long association with Baylor had come to a close. On November 19, 1907, he resigned from the board of trustees at Baylor to devote himself full-time to the work of the new seminary.[76]

THE BEGINNING OF SOUTHWESTERN BAPTIST THEOLOGICAL SEMINARY

The first meeting of the Board of Trustees was on November 11, 1907, in the assembly room of the Menger Hotel, San Antonio. Of the thirteen individuals named to make up the new board, seven were present. The group elected J. B. Gambrell as president of the board and formed a committee to secure a charter, constitution, and bylaws, as well as "The Article of Faith" that would be accepted and signed by members of the faculty.[77]

The second meeting of the trustees took place three days later at First Baptist Church, Dallas. Carroll, still listed as dean of the seminary, led a discussion pertaining to the organization and endowment of the school. He informed the trustees that by Texas law the seminary could legally have up to twenty-five trustees instead of the thirteen that they presently had. Carroll recommended and the board approved twelve additional men to serve. The significance of this event cannot be overlooked. Carroll, who was president of the newly founded seminary, had personally selected twelve men who

F. L. Carroll Library and Chapel, Baylor University. The first classes of the Seminary were held in this building.
— Courtesy Southwestern Baptist Theological Seminary Archives

Southwestern Baptist Theological Seminary student body, 1912–13.
— Courtesy Southwestern Baptist Theological Seminary Archives

Examining the future site of Southwestern Baptist Theological Seminary.
— Courtesy Southwestern Baptist Theological Seminary Archives

B. H. Carroll's office furniture on display at Southwestern.
— Courtesy Southwestern Baptist Theological Seminary Archives

Faculty of Southwestern in 1912.
— Courtesy Southwestern Baptist Theological Seminary Archives

Southwestern Campus grounds about 1914.
— Courtesy Southwestern Baptist Theological Seminary Archives

would be serving as trustees. In any institution the president is powerless to make major decisions without the support of the board. Carroll, as a result of the selection process, was now guaranteed the backing of half of Southwestern's board. At this same meeting the name of the seminary was changed from Baylor Theological Seminary to Southwestern Baptist Theological Seminary.[78]

In March and April of 1908 Carroll wrote a series of four articles dealing with the seminary and its charter. The second article, dated March 26, 1908, contained the proposed charter outlining the purpose of the seminary and defining its ties to the Baptist General Convention of Texas. When the committee wrote the section of the charter concerning trustees, it had the Whitsitt Controversy in mind in that it designated the convention to appoint the trustees.[79]

In Carroll's explanation of the charter he included a statement saying that "the seminary [should] teach the preacher on all lines of his education."[80] This statement, as well as others made by Carroll, led many to fear that he was planning to establish a literary department as part of the seminary. During their May 8, 1908, meeting, the trustees approved the charter. W. A. Pool made a motion to relieve the fear that a literary department would be established:

> Resolved that there is nothing in the Charter of the Seminary that allows the establishment of a literary college and that the Board has no purpose to establish such an institution.[81]

Carroll highlighted two other aspects of the charter that proved interesting: the seminary could offer special degrees and other states could financially support the seminary. The section which allowed the seminary to confer "such other degrees as it may warrant" allowed for Carroll to issue special degrees in his area, English Bible. Article Nine broadened the seminary's base of support by allowing Baptist state bodies outside of Texas the ability to support Southwestern and to share in the appointment of its trustees.[82]

During the November trustee meeting, Carroll presented a lengthy list of recommendations. Recommendation Seven stated, in part, that the Articles of Faith for the seminary would be the New Hampshire Confession of Faith with the exception of the word *invisible* which would be replaced with *particular*, thus highlighting individual Baptist churches. This change was no doubt a result of the Landmark influence in the Southwest. Recommendation Eight stated that "The Seminary shall confer no honorary degrees."[83] This recommendation is interesting as Carroll's title of "Doctor" was honorary. To this day Southwestern has issued no honorary degrees.

Concerning the board of trustees, Carroll recommended: "The President of the Seminary shall be a member of the board ex officio, but without power to vote. No other member of the Faculty shall be, in any way, a member of the Board."[84] This statement is intriguing for two reasons. First, Carroll would not need a vote to influence the board; his mere presence at a meeting was influence enough. Second, Carroll, as both a faculty member and trustee at Baylor, was able to influence the trustees to approve steps which led to the creation of Southwestern. Carroll did not want a faculty member of the seminary wielding the same power over him that he had attempted to wield over Brooks at Baylor.

The most interesting recommendation, however, concerned the faculty:

> Every full professor of the Seminary shall, on acceptance of office, subscribe to the Articles of Faith hereinafter set forth, and any serious departure therefrom in his teaching shall be considered ground for his resignation or for his removal by the trustees.[85]

This recommendation allowed the faculty to hold and to teach some beliefs that might differ from the Articles of Faith as long as these teachings were not a "serious departure." No doubt Whitsitt, as well as many Baptists in the East, wondered what Carroll considered to be a "serious departure." Another product of the Whitsitt Controversy, seen in this recommendation, was the trustees' power to remove a professor who was teaching something deemed by the trustees to be a "serious departure." At Southwestern the trustees could "sit in judgment."

MOVE TO FORT WORTH

Southwestern clearly needed a new home to avoid forever being overshadowed by Baylor. In an article dated April 2, 1908, Carroll stated that the seminary was beginning to consider a site and that "any place" in the state that would like to be considered should begin preparations now. His plan was to open the fall session of the seminary in its new location on October 1, 1909.[86]

Carroll had stated from the beginning that the seminary would consider any place in Texas, but the cities of Dallas and Fort Worth were the favored choices. Fort Worth immediately launched a campaign to bring the seminary there.[87] Dallas, although not as well organized, was also interested in having the seminary. Correspondence between George W. Truett and Carroll indicated that Truett had a particular site in mind for the seminary in Dallas' Oak Cliff section; however, the site was considered to be too small by Carroll. No other records of sites in Dallas receiving serious consideration exist.[88] Some have speculated that Southwestern did not move to Dallas due to the existence of Buckner's Orphan Home in the city, though R. C. Buckner himself recommended Dallas as a site for the seminary.[89] Carroll received several invitations to locate the seminary in other cities as well.[90]

On September 21, 1909, the board of trustees voted to move the seminary to Fort Worth, provided a proper site could be secured.[91] The location would not be merely a matter of prayer but a matter of finances as well. Fort Worth had agreed to raise a $100,000 bonus should the seminary choose to locate there. Carroll clearly stated that the seminary would not come if the money was not raised. He told W. D. Harris, the mayor of Fort Worth:

> Most of our professors have classes and responsibilities on their hands at Waco. I am going to leave my boy, Lee Scarborough, here for thirty days, and if you will back him and give him and your people a chance and do not raise $100,000, we will pass to another place and look elsewhere for God's guidance, with no criticism on your city, trusting that God will reveal his will.[92]

The trustees viewed five sites within the city before selecting one on the south side of Fort Worth, located "one half mile west and one quarter mile south from the bolt works at the end of Hemphill street car line and [running] up to the Santa Fe railroad track."[93] The property was described as:

> A thirty-acre site and one-half interest in 194 acres of the Winston land; ten acres outright and a half interest in ninety-nine acres of land, owned by H. C. McCart; a tract of twenty acres owned by W. D. Reynolds; a ten-acre tract owned by Matt S. Blanton; a twenty-acre tract owned by the heirs of J. T. Wright; a thirty-acre tract owned by the owners of the S. J. Jennings survey and another tract of fourteen acres owned by G. E. Tandy. Other parties unconditionally gave $4,000 cash and $3,000 additional upon certain conditions.[94]

Front view of construction of Fort Worth Hall in 1909.
— Courtesy Southwestern Baptist Theological Seminary Archives

Back view of construction of Fort Worth Hall in 1909.
— Courtesy Southwestern Baptist Theological Seminary Archives

Carroll's classroom in Fort Worth Hall.
— Courtesy Southwestern Baptist Theological Seminary Archives

Library in Fort Worth Hall.
— Courtesy Southwestern Baptist Theological Seminary Archives

Chapel Fort Worth Hall in 1914.
— Courtesy Southwestern Baptist Theological Seminary Archives

Seminary signed a contract to build the first building in March 1910. Fort Worth Hall was to have been completed in time for the opening of the fall session, but delays prevented it from being ready. When the 126 students who matriculated that year arrived on campus, they found only the unfinished basement and first floor of Fort Worth Hall. L. R. Scarborough later wrote:

> Some rooms were finished. The only roof we had on the building was the concrete floors above the first and second floors. We had no heating plant, no water system installed. We had to improvise our heat by putting stoves in the rooms and pipes out the windows. The story of sacrificing, doing without conveniences, waiting and working is a long, glorious one. Mrs. A. H. Newman was Superintendent of Fort Worth Hall. Her task was somewhat like Mrs. Noah's after the flood.[95]

CARROLL AS TEACHER

Carroll's approach to teaching was similar to his approach to preaching — to communicate clearly the truth of scripture as he understood it. Carroll's gifts of oration and communication, which served him well in the pulpit, were also assets in the classroom. The way in which he communicated his understanding of the Bible made the scriptures come alive for his students.

> He saw things and made others see them. The scenes of Bible history were as real to him as the scenes of his childhood. He could walk the streets of Jerusalem, Antioch, Ephesus, Athens, Corinth, and Rome with his students, reciting the history of these places and pointing out the celebrities of each, with as much ease apparently as if he had visited them the day before. His familiarity with the characters of the Bible was most remarkable. He talked of Abraham, Isaac, Jacob, Joseph, Moses, Joshua, Samuel, David, Solomon, John the Baptist, Jesus, and Paul as familiarly as he spoke of Houston, Baylor or Burleson.[96]

Carroll presented a variety of viewpoints on each subject that he taught. After briefly examining these positions, he spent the remainder of his lecture explaining his own view of the subject and why it was correct. He was so persuasive as a teacher that even the most obstinate student was often moved to adopt Carroll's position on any given subject.[97]

Students found note-taking to be difficult during Carroll's long and detailed lectures, which he delivered quickly. Their notebooks are filled with illegible handwriting and missing words. While Carroll clearly communicated his positions to his students, he did not make the recording of his positions easy.[98]

J. W. Crowder approached Carroll in the later years of his life about preserving his lecture notes. From these lectures Crowder has produced numerous books by Carroll. In fact, most of Carroll's influence through his written word today is attributed to Crowder's work in compiling and editing Carroll's notes.[99]

CARROLL'S FINAL YEARS

As Carroll's life drew to a close, he became aware of the fact that he had neglected his family during his ministry. While his son Guy lay near death in Carroll's Fort Worth home, Carroll often paced in front of his house, located at the present intersection of Stanley and Gambrell streets, muttering to himself: "I have taken care of the Lord's house, but not my own." Carroll admitted this neglect privately, but he never addressed the situation publicly.

Periods of poor health characterized the final years of Carroll's life from 1911 to 1914. Even before this time, Carroll spoke of the problems that his weak heart caused him.[100] His deteriorating health might have spelled doom for the young seminary had not Carroll persuaded a young preacher from Abilene to join the faculty. His name was L. R. Scarborough. As early as November 1906, Carroll tried to convince Scarborough to join the seminary as a professor of evangelism and field secretary.[101] Scarborough finally heeded Carroll's call in February 1908. In the next few years he would play a key role in the fundraising campaigns of the seminary.

As Carroll's health weakened, he sensed the need to fill the administrative void created by his inability to perform certain duties of the presidency. At the trustees' meeting in May 1913, Carroll requested the creation of the office of assistant to the president. He then recommended that L. R. Scarborough fill the position "in view of his thorough understanding of the work and duties of the president."[102]

During the final years of Carroll's life, a former student and long-time friend, J. Frank Norris, began to cause Carroll some irritation. Norris, through the pages of the *Baptist Standard*, was instrumental in arousing public support for the creation of the new seminary in 1907 and 1908. In 1909, just prior to Fort Worth's being

L. R. Scarborough.
— Courtesy Southwestern Baptist Theological Seminary Archives

chosen as the new location, Norris was called as pastor of the First Baptist Church of Fort Worth with Carroll's recommendation. After assuming the pastorate, Norris helped to lead Fort Worth in raising $100,000 for the seminary. He also served on the board of trustees from 1909 to 1915. When the doors of the new school opened, no stronger supporter existed outside of Carroll himself.

Norris had a mysterious, life-changing experience in 1911 while in revival in Kentucky. He vaguely alluded to it in a conversation with his wife while he was still in Kentucky:

> Wife, wife, we have had the biggest meeting you ever saw — more than half a hundred sinners have been saved, and they are shouting all over this country, and the biggest part of it is, wife, you have a new husband. He has been saved tonight, he is starting home and we are going to start life over again and lick the tar out of that crowd and build the biggest church in the world.[103]

Upon Norris' return to Fort Worth, he made sweeping changes at First Baptist Church, causing some members to leave. In February 1912, fire destroyed the church and the investigators charged Norris with arson. Later acquitted, Norris maintained leadership of the church, causing many to leave. G. H. Connell, knowing the influence that Carroll had with Norris, wrote to him asking for help. Connell reminded Carroll that Norris was called as pastor on Carroll's recommendation; therefore, Carroll should ask Norris to resign for the good of the church.[104] In response Carroll pleaded for patience, stating that Norris had indicated that he would resign at year's end. Norris did not do so; and many faculty members of Southwestern, including Carroll, left First Baptist Church.[105]

By the beginning of 1913, Carroll had to take action to keep Norris' activity on the board of trustees in check. H. Leon McBeth believes that only Carroll's forceful personality stopped Norris from attacking the seminary during Carroll's lifetime.[106] Had he lived longer, however, Norris eventually would have attacked his old friend, as well as the rest of the seminary. After the death of Carroll, Norris, who was once the seminary's closest friend, became its strongest enemy.

Though external controversy existed, the only serious internal conflict that the seminary experienced during this period was between Carroll and the faculty. However, Carroll may have been the only one to view the conflict as a problem. The controversy centered on Carroll's English Bible class. Because of his poor health and frequent absence from class, many students were unable to complete their required hours; therefore the faculty recommended that another course be substituted to fulfill the requirement.[107] Carroll was not in favor of this substitution. During a period from 1912 to 1913, when Carroll was in a coma and not expected to recover, A. H. Newman, dean of the faculty, and Professor J. J. Reeves worked on a plan to dismantle Carroll's Department of English Bible and integrate it into the Departments of Old Testament and New Testament. Carroll unexpectedly recovered; and upon learning of the plan, he called Newman and Reeves to his house and requested their resignations.[108] The power that Carroll had among the trustees, even in ill health, can be seen in the fact that they accepted the resignations of Newman and Reeves without discussion.

W. W. Barnes, who replaced Newman as professor of church history in 1913, provides a detailed account of an encounter with Carroll during his final year of life. Upon arriving in Fort Worth, Barnes met with Carroll. During the conversation Carroll pulled his trousers out to show the weight that he had lost. Barnes commented later that "you see the wreck of a man." Carroll asked Barnes many questions about Southern Seminary, from which Barnes had come. Afterward he explained his inquiries:

> I am trying to build a seminary and have never had any Seminary training. I do not know from personal experiences the inside life of theological seminaries. Therefore I am seeking information from every possible source.[109]

Carroll's third wife, Hallie Harrison, devoted much of her time during their fifteen years of marriage to the care of Carroll as his health declined. He called her his "angel of goodness" for the devotion that she showed him. Hallie was constantly at his side during his final months in order to ensure that his conversations and actions were not misunderstood.[110]

As Carroll neared death he remained concerned about the possibility of a regional split within the Southern Baptist Convention as reflected in a conversation with Scarborough: "This seminary will either be the center of a new convention composed of Southwestern states, or the Southern Baptist Convention will take over ownership and control." The latter occurred in 1925 when, with the legal technicalities worked out, the Baptist General Convention of Texas transferred ownership of the seminary to the Southern Baptist Convention.

DEATH OF B. H. CARROLL

B. H. Carroll died on November 11, 1914, in Fort Worth. In honor of his service to Texas Baptists, the *Baptist Standard* dedicated the entire November 19, 1914, issue to Carroll's memory. In announcing Carroll's passing, J. B. Gambrell wrote: "The tallest tree in the forest has been uprooted." George W. Truett, who as a young preacher assisted Carroll in raising money for Baylor and missions work, preached the funeral sermon. In the sermon, Truett said:

> Some other day, on some other occasion, I may speak out of my heart something of my personal feelings for him, but I dare not, cannot, will not do so today. Whose heart here today does not cry out as did Elisha when he watched the ascending Elijah, "My father, my father, the chariots of Israel and the horsemen thereof?"[111]

One of Carroll's greatest contributions to the Southern Baptist Convention surely would be his "discovery" of George W. Truett.

Other Texas Baptist leaders, such as J. B. Cranfill, L. R. Scarborough, George W. McDaniel, and Jeff D. Ray remembered the impact that Carroll's life had upon Baptists. Baptist newspapers around the country eulogized him. The *Baptist and Reflector* called Carroll "one of the greatest men of the South," saying that news of his death "sent a wave of sadness through our Southern Zion." The *Western Recorder* called Carroll's loss "serious" and stated that "his death dates the passing of the world's greatest Baptist."[112] In a candid and true assessment of Carroll's character, the *Religious Herald* wrote:

> While thoroughly amiable and loveable in temper, he was, nevertheless, too imperious in will to learn or use any of the arts of finesse. He had to move straight on to his subject, and it was usually a massive and almost relentless movement.[113]

The *Baptist Courier* speculated:

> His name will stand with the name of Boyce. The people of Texas will talk of him for fifty years to come. And so long as the Baptists of the South have a history so long will something be said of this great leader.[114]

Though Carroll was gone, his influence would continue through his books, his former students, and his seminary.[115]

CHAPTER 5

Carroll's Legacy

B. H. Carroll's influence as a national leader within the Southern Baptist Convention historically has been overshadowed by his founding of Southwestern Baptist Theological Seminary. As a result, many see Carroll as a regional leader of Southern Baptists, minimizing his role at the national level. His speech which helped to save the Home Mission Board has been virtually forgotten. His role in the founding of the Sunday School Board rarely receives mention. Even his role as the leader of the opposition to Whitsitt in the Whitsitt Controversy is often reduced to that of a disenchanted Baptist. B. H. Carroll preached at every convention he attended after 1878. Leaders of the convention realized the power of his words in shaping the opinions of many Southern Baptists. His correspondence reveals that men throughout the convention not only sought his friendship but his advice as well. Carroll's contemporaries in the eastern sections of the convention mentioned him in the same breath with men like John A. Broadus and James P. Boyce. Carroll was truly a national leader in the Southern Baptist Convention.

Although Carroll's leadership had an impact on the convention at the national level, his influence was strongest in Texas. Using his knowledge and his skill as a debater, Carroll communicated his positions clearly to Texas Baptists. His early success in the Fisher Debates made him the people's champion in Baptist orthodoxy, a role

123

that he would fill time and time again. Through his part in the Prohibition Movement, the Martin Controversy, the Hayden Controversy, and the Whitsitt Controversy, he standardized orthodoxy in Texas. His unique blending of Graves' theology and support of cooperative missions is still found in some Texas churches today. Ironically, however, Carroll's concern for orthodoxy often was not the main catalyst in prompting his involvement in these movements. He was in no hurry to confront M. T. Martin until Martin called him a "denominational boss." Carroll's conflict with the Marlin church had less to do with associational relationships than with the challenge to his authority. His reaction against Hayden was not just a defense of denominational missions but a personal battle against a strong adversary. In leading the fight to remove Hayden, Carroll also removed the only person with the influence to sway the thoughts of Texas Baptists against him. Carroll's leadership in the Whitsitt Controversy was not a result of his belief in church successionism but a result of the embarrassment that he felt after the trustee meeting at Wilmington. Thus on each of these occasions viewed by Texas Baptists as a fight for orthodoxy, Carroll's actual involvement was personally motivated.

As a Texas Baptist leader Carroll made one of his greatest contributions by fighting for the right of Texas Baptists to exist as equal partners in the Southern Baptist Convention. Speaking before the convention in 1888 in support of the necessity of the Home Mission Board and the need for mission aid in Texas, Carroll insisted at the same time that his home state must be accepted on equal terms with other states in the convention. When the East did not take the concerns of Texas seriously during the Whitsitt Controversy, Carroll brought the convention to the verge of a split to make his point that the beliefs of Texas Baptists, where the "soul of J. R. Graves marches on," must be accepted in order to have true unity in the convention.

Because of Carroll's powerful physical presence and stirring emotional appeal, his overall leadership style can be described as manipulative — but manipulative in order to achieve what he considered to be the best interests of his people. When Carroll felt his authority threatened at First Baptist, Waco, he manipulated the church into giving him even more authority through well-timed resignations. Perhaps the best example of Carroll's power to manipulate comes from the board meeting at Baylor in which he told of a vision to establish a new seminary. Whether or not the vision actually took place is not important; the way in which Carroll presented it and the impact that it had upon the trustees are reminiscent of Carroll's adventure into the haunted house as a small boy. How could the trustees of Baylor not vote to start a new seminary after Carroll's oration? They could not dare to question so clear a vision; and Carroll's presentation was so powerful that the board did not even pause before voting to start a new seminary, even with the president of the university absent.

Carroll not only appealed to others' emotions but was an emotional man himself. The same drive that he displayed when attacking the streetcar driver who had questioned his honor he displayed throughout his life in the causes that he led. There were very few times in Carroll's ministry when he was not involved in one fight or another; and sometimes he was engaged in two or three controversies at once. He almost always won. Carroll's lone major defeat, the Prohibition Movement, came in the political arena — but his honor remained intact. Even in his one major defeat, Baptists saw him working hard for a just cause.

Carroll's greatest contribution to Baptist life, as well as to American Christianity, was the founding of Southwestern Baptist Theological Seminary. Many men throughout history have been described as being ahead of their time, but B. H. Carroll was definitely a man of his time. In the founding of Southwestern Baptist Theological Seminary, he met one of the greatest needs of his time. In many respects the seed for Southwestern was planted at Independence with the creation of Baylor University in 1845, for one might argue that a seed for a theological seminary is planted with the founding of each Baptist school, just waiting for the ideal situation and the right person to arise to stimulate its growth. At the turn of the century Texas was the ideal situation, and B. H. Carroll was the right man to stimulate the growth of Southwestern's seed.

Carroll's close association with Waco University and then with Baylor University, his service on the board of trustees at Southern Seminary, and his long pastorate at First Baptist, Waco, helped to prepare him for his role as president of Southwestern Seminary.

Many factors contributed to the founding of Southwestern. The Whitsitt Controversy was one such factor, though not the primary catalyst; instead the controversy served to accelerate the natural evolution of ministerial training at Baylor. One of the major factors in Carroll's decision to establish Southwestern was the chance to correct "mistakes" that he believed existed at Southern Seminary when he served on the board there. For example, Carroll found during the controversy that little could be done if the trustees refused to act. He also discovered that many of the older, established states in the convention viewed the concerns voiced by frontier states, such as Texas, as unimportant. Therefore, in the founding of Southwestern, Carroll created an institution that would be aware of the concerns of regional Baptists and would be directly accountable to them.

Since many of the Baptists who supported Southwestern were "backwoods folk" and since Southwestern was located in a western state, many Baptists in the convention perceived the new seminary to be a school for "hillbillies" while Southern Seminary in Louisville was perceived to be a school for "refined" students. Unfortunately, remnants of this perception still exist today.

As a result of his work in founding Southwestern Seminary, Carroll paved the way for additional seminaries within the Southern Baptist Convention. In fact, the founding of Southwestern laid the groundwork for the regional seminary approach that the convention uses today.

When Carroll lay on his deathbed, the realization that he would no longer be able to guide the seminary must have been more painful than his illness. Although he had expressed confidence in Scarborough on many occasions, Carroll was undoubtedly concerned for the welfare of his institution in the absence of his watchful eye. Perhaps some of his final words of advice to Scarborough were as much an effort to calm Carroll's own fears about the seminary's future as they were to give guidance to his successor:

> My greatest concern is not for myself. My spiritual horizon is cloudless. . . . But my deep concern is about the Seminary. Your life will be given largely to it. It is an institution born in the prayer of faith and in the faith of prayer. You will need faith and prayer ahead.[1]

❖   ❖   ❖

> If heresy ever comes in the teaching, take it to the faculty. If they will not hear you and take prompt action, take it to the trustees of the Seminary. If they will not hear you, take it to the convention that appoints the Board of Trustees, and if they will not hear you take it to the great common people of our churches. You will not fail to get a hearing then.[2]

In reading accounts of Carroll's life and work as written by his contemporaries and former students, one finds depicted an almost superhuman champion of truth. While Carroll did champion the truth as he understood it, he was just a man with strengths and weaknesses like any other man; he had his own secret motives and hidden agendas which drove him to fight for various causes. His spirit and influence are preserved in the volumes of lectures, sermons, articles, and speeches collected by J. W. Crowder and J. B. Cranfill. Through these works one can catch a glimpse of the man whom many refer to as "a giant in Baptist life." Carroll's greatest character flaw was, ironically, his greatest strength: he never believed that he was wrong. As a result Carroll was always convicted of the rightness of his cause and the justness of his actions. He used his skill as a debater from the pulpit, on the convention floor, and in the boardroom and newspapers to expound on and support his beliefs and opinions. Although Carroll dominated meetings and conventions in an effort to accomplish his goals, without his single-minded commitment Southwestern Seminary would not have become a reality nor would his life and work have been ensconced in the pantheon of Baptist leaders.

Introduction to Appendices

B. H. Carroll had a multifaceted ministry as a denominational leader, pastor, and seminary president. The three addresses which comprise the appendices provide a glimpse of how Carroll perceived each of his roles.

Appendix One is Carroll's address on the Home Mission Board delivered before the Southern Baptist Convention in 1888. As stated earlier, many who were at the meeting credit Carroll's address with ending questions on the need for the Home Mission Board. Within the text Carroll hints at regional divisions in the Southern Baptist Convention which will become more evident during the Whitsitt Controversy in the late 1890s. His parallel between Texas' sending her young men to fight for the South during the Civil War and his call to the Southeast to send her money and young men to Texas for missions work is a poignant reminder of the emotions stirred in remembering the war as well as the importance that Carroll placed upon Home Missions.

Appendix Two is Carroll's farewell address to the First Baptist Church of Waco on January 1, 1899, a church he had pastored for twenty-eight years. The address reveals the bond that had developed between Carroll and his congregation. The times of controversy and disagreement are forgotten as Carroll expresses his love for the church. He refers only vaguely to his prior resignations at First Baptist by stating that his resignation is not designed "to call forth some additional expression of endorsement of affection from you or to induce you to do a certain thing." In a brief moment of self-reflection, Carroll notes that he never filled some of his pastoral duties well, especially in the area of visitation. He ends the address abruptly by stating, "Why did God so fully restore my health and renew my desire to live?" To those who heard the address then or read it now the answer is clear — Carroll's health and desire were renewed in order that he might face new challenges.

Appendix Three is Carroll's address to the first graduating class of Southwestern Baptist Theological Seminary in 1908. Carroll reminds the graduates that the world will judge Southwestern by their lives. He states, "The supreme test of every institution is its work, embodied not in theory but in living men, whose lives illustrate its value." While the success of their ministries will help to establish Southwestern's reputation, the graduates are challenged to do even more for their school. At the close of his address, Carroll announces that he will spend the summer traveling in order to raise money for the new seminary. He challenged every graduate to contribute to the school, concluding with a veiled threat, "While you may forget, I shall recall these words at the end of the summer, and look over the names of the graduates of this day and make a record of the responses to this plea."

Appendix I

Dr. Carroll's Farewell Address to His Church
Sunday Morning Jan. 1, 1899

Brethren & Sisters of the First Baptist Church at Waco:

Twenty-eight years ago, this day, by your own free and unanimous election, I became your pastor. This proceeding was neither hasty nor inconsiderate on your part or mine, but followed a year's service as pulpit-supply, which afforded opportunity for that mutual acquaintance most helpful to a proper ratification of an engagement the most solemn and sacred on earth next to the marriage tie. This highest honor and office in the gift of men you conferred on me, when I was young, inexperienced, every way distrustful of my ability to meet the requirements of so great a responsibility, but trustful that your charity would cover a multitude of faults and that your kind forbearance would patiently endure many shortcomings.

But above all was my reliance upon the Shepherd and Bishop of Souls, who through the Holy Spirit, makes men overseers of his flock, and keeps open, day and night, forever, the door of access to the throne of Grace, that through prayer and supplication, both pastor and people, may obtain wisdom for guidance and find help in every time of need.

As at my recent birthday, only last Tuesday, I was fifty-five years old, it follows that more than half my life I have ministered to you.

And today — "a day of memory and tears" — when I survey in one sweeping retrospect the whole circle of events and experiences. What a panorama of vicissitudes fills my vision and moves my heart!

What an alternation of joys and sorrows — of greetings and partings! Like a succession of lights and shadows they glide before me and silently beckoning steal away, swift and returnless, into the dead and buried past.

131

Since that first of January, twenty-eight years ago, a generation has come and gone. Fathers and mothers have fallen asleep. Children born to me, and to many of you, have grown to maturity and become responsible heads of their own families.

In that time also, "oft have death and sorrow reigned" in your homes and mine. More than half of my own household sleep in your cemeteries — waiting for the resurrection. If I were to die today I would find in heaven to greet me more of my family, and perhaps more of my congregation, than remain on earth. How through a subtle trick of memory do the scenes group and shift themselves. Side by side appear the cradle and grave — in one an infant coos and smiles while the pastor invokes divine blessing on the beginning of a new life — in the other the Saint reposes, where the wicked cease from troubling and the weary are at rest. I see a host of fair maidens and brave young men plighting their vows of love and fidelity before me at the marriage altar — and more precious than all glorious meetings of strongest power in which Souls are born anew — Saints confirmed — Sorrows healed — differences adjusted — and "Heaven comes down our Souls to greet While Glory crowns the Mercy-Seat." Very far is it from my present purpose to review the work of all these years, but I cannot refrain from bare allusions to some facts which greatly mitigate the pain in my heart this day because of some other things to be said afterwards.

Foremost of these is the fact that in my whole pastorate there has never been a church trouble. Here, if I may modestly state it, has been my most valuable service as a pastor. Ah! me, eternity alone can disclose to you how I have watched over your welfare on this point. Whatever the tension — whatever the case of discipline — whatever the opportunity for bitterness strife or division — through it all by God's grace you have been led on all occasions of hazard into practical and peaceful unanimity. Second, it refreshes my heart this day to recall that I never urged you into an enterprise without taking the lead, nor to incur an expense which I did not liberally share. And you are my witnesses that always when many needs cried for precedence in supply I have urged you, yea many times over-persuaded you, to count your financial obligations to me as least important and last to be considered. And whatever delay has been on your part in this matter at any time is but the result of the pastor's teaching, leaving you void of reproach. When the famous Indian chief, Tecumseh, was asked to state the relative merits of two noted British commanders with whom he had served as an ally, he tersely replied: "General Proctor always said, Tecumseh, *You* go — but General Brock always said, Tecumseh, *We* go."

I am sure I have never played the *role* of General Proctor with you.

Third, it fills me with amazement and gratitude to be able to recall no instance — not one — in twenty-eight years, wherein you refused or failed to do just what your pastor asked you to do. Sometimes, indeed, I have suspected that you differed from me somewhat as to the wisdom, expediency or extent of a measure proposed, but you never faltered — always when I came down from the pulpit, stood close to you and looking earnestly into your eyes asked you for Christ's Sake to do any thing *[sic]* — most lovingly you did it.

Finally, I can but rejoice that under my administration, you have taken a foremost place among the churches of the world in every good mark.

So that the stream of your influence for good has not been dammed up into a narrow, shallow, local, stagnant pool, but has out-flowed to many lands and cheered a thousand distant wastes.

In the light of these four general facts how strange is it that I must now abruptly say: Brethren I tender you my resignation as pastor to take effect *at midnight last night.*

Such action on my part must naturally awaken inquiry. It will be generally felt in the state among our people as well as in your hearts that only the gravest reasons will justify such a step. The situation calls for explanation — prompt and adequate explanation to guard against misconstruction hurtful to me — and what is far more important hurtful to you.

To clear away the brush of any harmful supposition that may arise I will first answer, in order, some possible questions:

1. Is it the object of this resignation to call forth some additional expression of endorsement of affection from you — or to induce you to do a certain thing — or any way looking to your recalling me to office under conditions more satisfactory than exist? My answer is an emphatic No. Such an unmanly expedient, unworthy of both you and me, I am incapable of practicing. The resignation is sincere meaning just what its terms import to an honest, candid mind.

2. Is it called forth by a conviction on my part that the congregation desires a change? I do not believe such desire exists. Always the deacons have been changed on their honor as men of God to apprise me promptly of even the smallest indications of such desire, on the assurance that the bond which unites us as pastor and people must be a rope of Sand when they want it broken. If men are capable telling the truth there is no such reason for my resignation. On the contrary, I have abundant and recent reason to believe that the Severance will be as sad to you as to me.

3. Is it prompted by any grievance on my part against the church? In the name of my Redeemer, and as if an oath before his judgment bar — I answer that I have no grievance, under heaven, against this church, and no complaint of ill-treatment. Last night when my mind went back over all these years to see if anything in your conduct towards me was blameworthy, while the tears ran down my face, my heart spoke out — Nothing — nothing whatever. Indeed, when I stand before the white throne of the final judgment I will want to testify before the universe of men and angels and God himself, that one church, at least, for 28 years, never wronged its

pastor. Indeed, I do not believe there exists on earth today another church whose unvarying goodness to its pastor surpasses yours.

There may possibly be some small fault of yours towards me — but my love — my deep undying love — cannot see a spot. And when I think of all this in connection with the profound consciousness of my own shortcomings towards you my heart melts within me.

No partisan friend of mine can have or shall have warrant of censure against you on my account, because I have no real or supposed grievance. Brethren, I stand before you a perjured man, if you are not guiltless — white as Sorow [sic] in this regard — at the bar of my heart.

4. Is it because having been for years giving much attention to general denominational work, I feel that I cannot take up again the details of pastoral work? This to an honest mind is a harder question than the others, when we consider the tremendous power of a long habit. And yet, after prayerful reflection, I must again answer, No. I do believe I could and would resume pastoral duties, at least as well as I ever did — never having been at my best much of general visitor of my people in their homes.

5. Is it because for other reasons I wish to leave Waco? Most assuredly no, since I am conscious of neither desire or purpose to leave Waco until God calls me to a heavenly home. My earthly home is here. My dead are here and by their side I wish to be buried when I die. My citizenship is here. For Waco's best interests as I have understand them, I have labored twenty-nine years and expect to continue the service through the remnant of my days. Above all my church is here — a church dearer to me than any other on this earth — dearer than any other can be. It is my purpose to retain my membership and to be a helper in its all its, and announce now my purpose to contribute $100 a year to any pastor you may call.

And when at home hold myself in readiness to render any service you may require.

6. Is it because I no longer desire to be your pastor? Again, without the shadow of reservation I answer, No. Every inclination of my heart is to remain your pastor and end my days in your service. Not to do it nearly breaks my heart. Most fervently do I pray that none of you may suffer as I suffer in the severance of this bond.

Then, what can be the occasion of the resignation? You have a right to know. There is no mystery about it. It is simply a matter of conscience. To lead up to the cause I now and answer a seventh question:

7. Is it because you feel in your heart you *could not* close your ear to other outside calls for help? Here I am compelled to answer, Yes. Constituted as I am, loving all the cause as I do, well do I know that when the voices are loud enough, and the need urgent, and the cause in peril is sufficiently — then I would be sure to hear them. They would come to me by night as the man of Macedonia came to Paul. They would stand by me and drive off sleep by crying: "Come over and help *Us*." And as when in re-

versal of Homer's story Greece thus appealed for help to Troy, Paul yielded — leaving Asia to carry the gospel to Europe — so I would yield.

But it may be objected, why not wait for the voices. My answer is I have already heard them. Then, why not, as hertofore [*sic*] heed the voices, remaining pastor here? Therein is the gist of the whole matter, the circumstances have changed. When heretofore you so generously released me to do general denominational work there was no other remedy. The state of the case was such in past junctures that was thus done had to be at the sacrifice of some church. Nothing else then could have availed. It is not so now. Such a crisis in denominational affairs no longer exists. Moreover, if it did exist, you are no longer able to make the sacrifice without very serious harm to the church. You need a pastor's attention and heart and time. You need him now and need him much. You cannot afford longer to be without his services at home. But rather than [surrender] the present pastoral relation would it not be better to release for a limited [time] only, as heretofore. Again we reach the gist of the matter. Because in this last case of appeal from without a limited period of absence *[sic]* will not meet the requirements of the case. Again I borrow the philosophy of an Indian chief. In the old French and Indian war, when Sir William Johnson heard of the near approach of Baron DisKean at the head of a formidable force of French and Indians, and had determined to send out 200 men to feel the enemy, he asked the judgment of his ally, Hendricks, the famous Indian chief. The characteristic reply was: "If you send the 200 men to be slaughtered, they are too many. If you send them to accomplish good in this case, they are too few."

Applying the illustration, I can do no Material good by *touching lightly* the service which calls me from my pastorate. It is too great a service for incidental aid and its needs and perils too urgent for delay. In my deliberate judgment, wrapped up in the success of the cause calling for my aid, is the well-being of our whole denomination for a hundred — perhaps a thousand years to come.

As Lyman Beecher — the greatest of all the Beecher's once said in substance: "If that great ship goes down a thousand smaller vessels will be swallowed up in its vortex."

What then is this great cause?

I refer to Christian Education as embodied in the mark of the Texas Baptist Education Commission. If that cause fails we may not expect to regain a hearing of the people not to restore public confidence. When it collapses down go all our Schools and colleges. When it succeeds they rest on enduring foundations. In the general cause of Christian education is involved the work of the Bible-Department of Baylor University, which more than any other on agency possesses the Solution of the thousand ills which have heretofore afflicted and cripple us.

But as my present purpose is served more by the statement of a fact than the elaboration of an argument, I defer to a later day and reserve for a wider audience a discussion of the merits of the cause whose voice of help I have so distinctly heard.

And now brethren allow me to remind you that only recently your prayers without cooperation on my part, plucked me from the Jordan of Death when I was gladly yielding myself to its swelling flood.

Why did God so fully restore my health and renew my desire to live?

Appendix II

Address to the First Graduating Class of
Southwestern Baptist Theological Seminary

Obvious circumstances preclude such an address as this first class deserve, and which it would delight me to make under more favorable conditions. The people, the teachers, and the student body are worn-out with the long-continued commencement exercises held in the city by many institutions.

My words, therefore, will be few. You, young men, and brother ministers, go out as the advance guard of what we trust shall be a great army. It devolves on you, the pioneer representatives of the Seminary, to make the first impression on the public mind of the value of our theological work.

Your character as honorable men, your piety as Christians, your wisdom and efficiency as ministers of our Lord, may accredit your Alma Mater to the whole world, but the absence or opposites of these qualifications will certainly bring on it incalculable discredit. The supreme test of every institution is its work, embodied not in theory but in living men, whose lives illustrate its value.

There is no argument against good fruits — and none can buttress evil fruits. In a large measure you carry on your banners the future of ministerial education in the Southwest. By your lives and deeds you will either advertise its failure or vindicate its wisdom.

A good interpretation of one of Paul's sayings declares: "The woman shall live in her children if they continue in faith and love and sanctification with sobriety." But a mother dies in the shame of unworthy children.

He also contended that he needed no letters of commendation as some others, but that his converts were his living letters of commendation, known and read of all men. Even our Lord himself will be admired in the people he saves and uplifts from bondage and death to a complete salvation. How much more then must an Alma Mater live in her alumni and be glorified in them.

I burden your minds, already surfeited with commencement exercises, with only one charge and one plea. The charge is: Remember that you go out as constructive and not destructive factors. Open therefore your hearts very wide to all the varied interests of the Kingdom of God. Rejoice at opportunity to serve any good. You will misrepresent the Seminary if you do not positively and aggressively support every enterprise favored by our State Convention and our Southern Baptist Convention. Particularly are you, as beneficiaries, under bonds to befriend our Education Commission which seeks the higher efficiency of all our correlated schools, with emphasis on loyalty to Baylor University in view of what it has done for you.

The one plea assumes not the form of a charge. In the most tender, tactful, and delicate letter ever written by Paul, he says to Philemon: "Wherefore, though I have all boldness in Christ to enjoin thee that which is befitting, yet for love's sake, I rather beseech, being such a one as Paul the aged, and now a prisoner also of Christ Jesus; I beseech you for Onesimus, my child, whom I have begotten in my bonds."

The application should occur to you, without an external hint. You well know what I regard as the crowning mission of my life; what to me is more than life, and that is to see the Southwestern Baptist Theological Seminary extablished on such a basis as will insure perpetuity and place it among the greatest training schools for preachers in this world. Never more inspiring incentives.

I may not say with Campbell's wizard:

> 'Tis the sunset of life gives me mystical lore,
> And coming events cast their shadows before.

Nor may I claim the spirit of prophecy, but I do feel, brethren, on my heart, like unquenchable fire, that I have been thrust out by God to lay the foundations of this institution which, in my judgment, will largely influence the Kingdom of God in the Southwest. I may plead, then, gently knocking at the door of your hearts, in terms of persuasion, not command.

Believe me when I say that the crisis of this institution is in this summer. The Seminary seeks endowment and a home. My age admonishes me that I cannot wait for a more opportune season. I am not without due sympathy for other interests claiming public attention. But I feel that before we meet again this battle will have been won or lost. In these three summer months lies the great issue.

The Ancients had a saying concerning anything of the future: "It is on the knees of the gods." Unfortunately in this period I may not expect the co-operations of many leaders charged with other interests. I must expect that campaigns in behalf of these other interests will fill the vision of the hearts of many of our people. Some will be for us only in passive acquiescence. A few will be for us positively and indefinite deed. Every man of that few can do somewhat, something definite, something originated and consummated by himself.

If in these three months any of you, our first alumni, should chance in the press of other matters to remember what responsibility, what concern of heart, what labor, what loneliness rests upon him who loved, labored, and sacrificed in your behalf, and if in so remembering you should be led to prayer, and so praying, should be guided to do some real, positive, definite thing great or small, helpful toward victory, then you may be assured of the most grateful appreciation upon my part. While you may forget, I shall recall these words at the end of this summer, and look over the names of the graduates of this day and make a record of the responses to this plea.

Appendix III

Dr. B. H. Carroll

His Speech at Richmond, Va., Before the Southern Baptist Convention, in the Interest of the Home Mission Board and Vindicating its Appropriations to Texas, Saturday, May 12, A.D., 1888.

Bro. President and Brethren of the Southern Baptist Convention: A Northern writer has said: "There are but two States in the American Union with a past rich enough in historic lore and romantic legend to furnish a theme for an epic poem grander than the Illiad *[sic]* of Homer or the Eneid of Virgil. These States are Texas and Virginia."

From one of them, the most western in the territory of the Southern Baptist Convention, I come to-night for the first time in life, to stand upon the soil of the other, the most eastern in our bounds, to plead the cause of the Home Mission Board and to vindicate the wisdom of its missionary operations.

In the beginning, allow the statement of three propositions:

1st. The argument which necessitates the perpetuity of the Southern Baptist Convention, necessitates the perpetuity of its Home Mission Board.

2d. The facts of the present and the reasonable probabilities of the future call for an enlargement rather than a diminution of the work of this Board.

3d. The days will be few between the death of the Home Board and the death of the Foreign Board. The loss of either would be like severing the ligature which bound the Siamese Twins into a common, mutual and reciprocal life.

If these propositions be demonstrable, then to speak for the Home Board is to speak in behalf of the Foreign Board. To advocate the Home Board is to stand guard over the life of the Convention itself.

Conversely: to attack or depreciate the Home Board is, whether unconsciously or designedly, to assail the Foreign Board and to undermine the foundations of the Convention itself.

While the time allotted at this hour may not be sufficient to substantiate all these propositions, I, for one, desire to put myself on record, as being fully persuaded of their soundness, and they are susceptible of easy and overwhelming demonstration.

While the dangers which threaten the Home Board are not at present so imminent and formidable as in the past, yet there are even now difficulties which if they do not endanger its perpetuity do seriously embarrass its efficency *[sic]*, and by just so much lower the heart beat of life in the whole convention.

Let a citation of facts, collected from the report of the Board just submitted to this Convention introduce some of these difficulties. It appears from this report, printer's copies of which have been furnished to you all, that Alabama, Georgia, Kentucky, South Carolina, Tennessee and Virginia, without receiving back any appropriations, have together contributed to this Board during the past year $27,000. But Arkansas, Cuba, the District of Columbia, Florida, Louisiana, Maryland, Missouri, Mississippi, North Carolina and Texas, while making contributions have also received appropriations from the Board.

Now, one of the chief difficulties refered *[sic]* to, is the ignorance in the contributing States of the reality and the magnitude of the destitution in the receiving States and Territories. If there be some knowledge, vague and imperfect, there is no such realization of the facts in the case as creates a personal interest, enkindles enthusiasm and prompts intelligent contributions commensurate with the interest involved. I mean to affirm that a most cursory conversation with even the members of this Convention, presumably better informed than their respective constituencies, will disclose the most alarming lack of information concerning the necessities of the fields to which we are making small and, if you will excuse me, automatic contributions.

While this ignorance is notable concerning the destitution and the true situation in the cis-Mississippi States, it is stupendous and lamentable concerning the trans-Mississippi department.

One of the causes of this ignorance is the silence of our religious newspapers.

While I would not in this matter incriminate one more than another, yet as most of the editors present are far from their own domiciles, and like myself look a little homesick, I will confine my illustration to the Religious Herald of Richmond. I do this because here "McGregor is on his native heath," and buttressed by admiring friends. Because my own partiality for that great journal and friendship for its editors will strip criticism of sinister motive, and because the Herald can afford a few hard knocks from a friendly hand when crowned with merited laurels [sic] and buried under deserved eulogiums.

But to make a specific point: When the Convention was held in my city I took under the shelter of my humble foro forty Texas delegates, that you brethren from abroad might have the best places. One day I invited the Virginia editor to come and break bread and eat salt with us. To compensate him for such kindness, I induced every Texas delegate there that day to subscribe for the Religious Herald, and marked the promising blandness of his smile as he pocketed the shekels.

It is hoped that the Lord will forgive me for the stories I told those innocent delegates about what a great Texas paper the Herald was going to be.

Well, as time rolled on we began to scan the columns of our new Texas paper for the rich array of State items. I mean not fulsome compliments to our pastors of over-wrought pictures of Texas greatness, but such a presentation of the facts concerning the reality and magnitude of destitution as would justify and call forth the assistance of our more fortunate brethren and vindicate the wisdom of the appropriations made by the Atlanta Board.

Imagine then our surprise (I speak not of an exception here nor there) when we came to the average issue of the paper to find under great big capitals "News from Texas," just such news as this: "Young John Doe was married and old Mrs. Richard Poe was buried."

A regular tadpole, catfish arrangement — all head and no body. It reminded us of what one of the Herald's great editors — the lamented J. B. Jeter — once said of Alexander Campbell's promised reply to his history of Campbellism: "What a tremendous portico for such small house."

On one occasion, after reading these Texas items, a certain pastor in that State said, "Well, wife, you needn't wait to get the baby to sleep; let us kneel down right now and here and pray to the Lord to have mercy upon the soul of the man that gets up the Texas items for the Religious Herald."

Let another collection of facts from the report in your hands introduce another difficulty. From that report let us make out and consider the following table:

States	Contributed to the Board	Received
Arkansas	$ 126.00	$1,665.00
District of Columbia	203.00	500.00
Florida	22.00	2,700.00
Louisiana	167.00	2,592.00
Texas	1,624.00	7,235.00
Indian Territory	0	3,773.00
Maryland	5,878.00	751.00
Mississippi	924.00	623.00
North Carolina	1,803.00	600.00

Well, I had gotten thus far in my table when they said: "Come to supper; it is nearly time for the Convention to meet."

Anyhow, it goes far enough to show four classifications:

1st. Some States give and receive back nothing.

2d. Some States give more than they receive back.

3d. Some States give less than they receive back.

4th. One Territory receives, but gives back nothing.

In justice, I ask you to mark well that the amounts in this table as given by the several States do not include either what is raised by their local Boards for State work or what is done in co-operations with this Convention, but only what is given directly to the Atlanta Home Board.

This being understood, the facts elicited and tabulated enable us to comprehend the next difficulty as expressed somewhat is this fashion:

Why should old Virginia, that receives nothing from the Home Board, contribute money through that Board to great big Texas?" or "Why should little South Carolina give money to Arkansas?"

I think these questions illustrate if they do not express the difficulty. Now, unless this difficulty can be fairly and effectually removed the work of the Board is greatly impeded. When the difficulty becomes general the Board is dead.

Let it then be my supreme purposes in this hour to address myself to the removal of this difficulty. To show the fallacy of the objection couched in the question. In order to do this it is necessary to consider, not so much what to say as to say what I have to say that the words will smite men's consciences, find lodgment in their hearts and pierce them as with barbed arrows that cannot be extracted.

The brevity of time allotted will preclude a discussion of the whole field of destitution. Whatever might be said in behalf of that destitution in Florida, Louisiana, Arkansas and other lands to which appropriations of all, as I know more of it than of any other State, and as what is said of it will apply in a large measure to the others and is designed for such application may be allowed, I trust, to speak mainly of our State. From the Red River to the Gulf and from the Sabine to the Rio Grande, I know it. Its people and their customs have been my study. On its frontiers I have served as a ranger to beat back the ruthless savage. Where now are cities and great populations we once kindled our camp fires far from the sight and sound of human habitations. And in its armies I have served and suffered on the battle scarred plains of other States. And knowing Texas, you will let me speak of Texas.

At the outset, then, let me meet another objection made upon the floor of this Convention by a brother from South Carolina. The point of the objection is this: South Carolina does her own State Mission work without help from the board, and hence is entitled to only one delegate to every $500 so contributed, while Texas, through the aid of South Carolina's money, does her State Mission work in co-operation with the Home Mission Board, and thereby secures one delegate for every $100 contributed to this work. Thus the very benevolence of South Carolina and the destitution of Texas make a discrimination of basis of membership against the giver and in favor of the receiver. For instance, in this very Convention, by such basis of representation, Texas is entitled to more than 250 delegates.

To all which it affords me pleasure to say that in theory the brother's objection is most just, but in practice is wholly unnecessary. For consider these facts: Outside of her work of co-operation, so objectionable to the brother as a basis of representation, Texas was entitled to 77 delegates for her contributions to Foreign Missions and to 16 delegates for her direct contributions to the Home Board, making 93 in all. But she has actually on the floor of this Convention only 51 delegates. So it appears that she has not claimed representation for cooperation work, and would not do so unless you hold another meeting in Waco. Then indeed they would come up like ancient Israel to her national feasts, not to out vote the smaller delegations from other States, but to welcome them and to admire the glory of God in South Carolinians and Virginians.

At any rate, we will join the brother from South Carolina in removing that justly objectionable basis of representation, provided our great and good brother, H. H. Harris, from Virginia will never again explain that basis of representation by saying: "We that are strong ought to bear the infirmities of the weak."

How could he say that it was "the most unkindest cut of all."

Brethren, we don't ask you to bear our "infirmities." We, that are here, or those who sent us do not ask you to support our "weakness." Your money does not come to us. It goes where we are not. Of the $7,235 you appropriate to Texas, we give $1,624 and then add to it $1,700 more and send it to those great imperial domains in Texas where we are not. Let me suppose a case for my Palmetto brother. Suppose there was a spot of destitution in South Carolina, about twice as big as Virginia before it was divided, would it be wise to leave the rest of South Carolina to carry that burden alone? I repeat, your money is not given to us. My own Association for many years has sent all of its mission contributions out of her own bounds to the regions beyond. And if there should lie contiguous to our Association a spot of destitution something near the size of the Desert of Sahara or the empire of Austria, is that our "infirmity" because it is a part of Texas?

Allow me then to answer the question. "Why should our States over here send gospel aid to Texas?"

1st. My first argument is "red like crimson." It is an argument of blood. There was a time when Texas was not invaded. The hoof of an enemy's charger crushed no blade of grass on her prairies. No conflagrations of war made her skies lurid. No hostile flag waved over her towns. No gunboats ascended her rivers. No pestilence of famine stalked after the war god through her fertile fields. No charred chimneys stood like sentinels of desolation to mark the devastation of an invader. It is true a Federal fleet held for a short time an island on our coast, but a few Texas cavalrymen soon captured the fleet.

It is true a little spurt of an invasion crept up the Sabine river, but 25 or 40 of the boys blew it out of the water.

It is true after your armies had surrendered there was a little affair out near Matamoras *[sic]* or Brownsville, in which a few victorious cowboys fired the last shot of the war between the States.

It is true when Appomatox *[sic]* was followed by Johnson's surrender, that Kirby Smith, though no enemy was in a thousand miles, sent our boys home, but we disbanded even then somewhat like Adam went out of Paradise, just to be with Eve.

But when you called for help, when McClelland's "On to Richmond!" was out here in sight, there was no complaint of the largeness of the Texas delegation then. Mechanicsville, Beaver Dam, Gaines Mill, Cold Harbor, Frazer's Farm and Malvern Hill cannot speak to-day without calling the roll of the Texas dead. From the first Manassas to Appomatox *[sic]*, our raged battalions interposed their battle-thinned lines between the invader and the homes of your wives and daughters. All around you to-day in unmarked graves, without an epitaph, sleep Texas fathers and husbands whose own homes saw them no more forever. From their silent graves the ghosts of these heroes rise up before this Convention and say: "Virginians, we gave our lives for your wives and children. Is it a great thing that you should send the Gospel to our widowed and orphaned ones?"

On what mountain, in what valley of the South has not the Texan died? The soil all around your Home Board at Atlanta is fertile with their blood.

Shiloh, Vicksburg, and Chickamauga preserve their memory. Their battle yells yet echo in the mountains of Tennessee and Kentucky.

Because therefore Texas made common cause with you in your hour of peril, make it with us now in our time of need.

Once, when the infamous Port Bill environed Boston to crush out her commercial life, and when the bayonet of Gage was at her throat, Virginia sounded the tocsin of war and sent her batallions *[sic]* to help a sister commonwealth. For this you took great credit to yourselves both then and in history since. How then can you deny the Texan's plea of blood?

2d. My next argument is that your children are with us in Texas. You cannot withhold the bread of life from your own flesh and blood. My first pastoral charge was a colony of Virginians. They came over in a body from one of the churches of Andrew Broaddus, Jr. He preached them a farewell sermon before they left Virginia. And well do I recall how they would read to me the manuscript of that sermon, and patting me on the head would proudly say: "Ah! Sonny, you'll never preach like that till you live awhile in old Virginia." And in truth, Bro. President, I am mortally afraid that though I am here at last at the fountain of ministerial inspirations, I shall never be able to preach like Andrew Broaddus, junior or senior.

My second pastoral charge was a colony of Mississippians. A church moved over but left their pastor behind.

My present charge is made up of blue-blooded Virginians, Georgians, Kentuckians and Carolinians. Perhaps every Southern State has a representative in the congregation. But while you people come, you keep your preachers back. I never was more amused than when reading the proceeding of your last State gatherings and noticed how you exhausted all possible expedients to keep Virginia preachers at home. Your reports were wonderfully doleful and lugubrious. But you hesitated not in the meantime to reach out to all lands and to cull the excellent of the earth to supply your Richmond pulpits. And with your good people you also sent to Texas shores every ecclesiastical crotchet, every tangled theological had (no allusion to the Dallas pastor), made and bred from Dismal and Okefinokee swamps to the lagoons of Louisiana. And keeping back the Orthodox divines that banished these heterogeneous incongruities, you say: "Go over to those Texas preachers and become homogeneous; anything will do over there."

And then to cap the climax you claim our brightest boys and girls for your colleges and modestly ask our Texas patrons to pour the golden cost of education into the laps of your educators. Let us have reciprocity, brethren.

3d. My third argument is that when a foe invaded Texas, more terrible than Sheridan or Grant — a foe fouler *[sic]* than the vampire or the octopus — when Texas was in a death struggle with an adversary whose victories were sadder and bloodier than the Alamo or Goliad, your sister States, (I mean not these brethen *[sic]* here) but your fellow citizens, not only sent us no help, but raised large sums of money for the treasury of Alcohol, that he might buy up, browbeat and dominate a free Texas election. Ah! in that deadly strife Kentucky was "the dark and bloody ground" to us.

We helped you against Chicago. You helped Chicago and Milwaukee against us. My point is this: Shall Kentucky whisky *[sic]* be forced on us, and shall we be denied Kentucky gospel? Shall Kentucky liquor dealers donate their thousands to debauch us, and Kentucky Christians begrudge a few hundreds to save us?

Has not Texas some uses besides furnishing a market for Virginia tobacco and Kentucky whisky *[sic]*?

4th. Another argument lies in the strategical importance of Texas. It is not an idle statement that when you lose Texas you lose the Southern Baptist Convention. Learn one significant fact from history. On one eventful day the Southern Confederacy received its mortal wound. After that it was but a lingering death. I refer to the 4th of July which brought the triple disaster of Helena, Gettysburg, and Vicksburg. The repulse of Holmes at Helena, Ark., was a calamity. The repulse of Lee at Gettysburg was a more dreadful misfortune, but the surrender of Pendleton at Vicksburg was an irreparable disaster. When that July sun went down in this triple cloud of war, the succeeding night wrapped her pall around a doomed Confederacy. The Mississippi became an impassable abyss between two severed parts, neither of which could live without the other.

And I say to you, that when you lose Texas and the Trans-Mississippi department, your Vicksburg has fallen!

Texas is your gateway to Mexico and the Pacific slope. Texas before the days of the Republic was an integral part of that Coahuila in whose capital Powell now preaches. So far as your Missions there, or at any point westward, are concerned, Texas is one yet with Coahuila and indivisible.

5th. I submit an additional argument in this form: Texas yields a hundred fold to missionary cultivation. It is one of the fixed priciples [sic] of God's justice that "The earth which drinketh in the rain that cometh oft upon it and bringeth forth herbs meet for them by whom it is dressed, receiveth blessings from God; but that which beareth thorns and briers [sic] is rejected, and nigh unto cursing whose end is to be burned."

By this principle let Texas as a field of missionary operations be tried. That it has yielded generously to rain, sunshine and cultivation I can prove, not by laborious and pains-taking argumentation, not by subtle metaphysical disquisitions, but by causing facts to stand up before you that speak for themselves. They are not dumb, swathed, desicated [sic] mummies; they are not stuffed rhetorical figures propped by elocution in an upright posture, but they are alive. Hearts of hope and love beat in their bosoms. Tongues of missionary fire rest on their heads. Here they are; look at them. One of them is A. J. Holt, not only the grandest superintendent of missions in the English-speaking world, but in the whole earth to day. There is another — you know him well — W. D. Powell, the most successful missionary of Jesus Christ today that uplifts the cross on a foreign shore. A tree which bears such fruit is a good missionary tree. You would hardly call them thorns and briers [sic]. And back of them I look at the pastors. I saw them smile as my gifted brother from Baltimore dicoursed [sic] Friday night of his "tenth for the Lord," and of his $500 average for pastoral salary. They know that a Texas pastor who does not give one-tenth of his income to God, is not in good standing. They know that the average salary fall below $500. Some of them here on this floor gave last year more than all their income. And that there is life in such people, look at their colleges. About two years ago they united. To-day Baylor University, at Waco, built since unification, surpasses Richmond College in buildings and students. While the Belton College would be glad of a just comparrison [sic] with Hollins or Staunton [sic]. And remember, we had no Joseph E. Brown to give his fifty thousand. No W. W. Corcoran helped us. No Vassar, no Colgate, no Peabody, no Vanderbilt stretched out a friendly hand. Those structures to-day embody the many small gifts of poverty. Some day yet, perhaps, the princes of wealth will help us. Then look at our capitol here and at Frankfort — but our capitol was built not indeed with money, for we had it not, but we did have a million or so sur-plus acres for a building fund. You ought to see it one time before you die. Next time you come we will show it to you as a sample of the granite that by millions is yet unquarried in our mountains. When you do see it you'll come back home and sell yours to some backwood county for a court-house. I mention these things to show what possibilities and potentialities are over there, latent now, but ready to be waked.

6th. My next argument is that Texas is the world in embryo. The peoples of the earth are there, and still they come. You have heard of Ger-many. You have read how united Germany under Van Moltke invaded France. You saw one wave of the tide smite Strasburg with the thunders of bombardment. How a mightier volume enveloped Metz. How yet another rolled resistlessly *[sic]* over Sedan burying McMahon and Monarchy. How the confluent floods environed Paris. Then you know something of Ger-many. Well, Germany has invaded Texas. Among some better things she brings to our shores her beer gardens, her rationalism and her Sabbath des-ecration. They are there to stay, and we have about concluded it is easier to convert them than to fight them. Other people have reached the same con-clusions before our time. Scandinavia is there, with her hordes of Swedes, Norwegians and Danes. The soft tongued Italian greets you there in every street from his huckster counter.

Japan contributes her quota. The almond-eyed Mongolian from the Celestial Empire, even the "Heathen Chinee *[sic]*, with his tricks that are vain," finds a home among us.

While all along a border longer than the entire circumference of sev-eral other States, the friendly Mexican comes over the Rio Gránde to vote in prohibition elections, for a consideration.

In the matter of population, Pentecost has come to Texas: "Men of every nation under heaven speak there in their own tongue, wherein they were born." Yes, Texas is the great white sheet, knit together at the four corners, and let down from heaven before this Convention, which is doubting Peter. While ever and anon some growling soul repeats: "Not so, Lord; not so, Lord!" When the statement is made by any man, whomso-ever, from "low-land or high-land, far or near," that Texas is not true Gos-pel missionary ground, I will not say that such a statement is a mistake, but I will say it is a hallucination of the devil.

Brethren, you do not know. You do not realize. If you knew yesterday you do not know to-day. The increase of population, and the development of material resources are appalling. And then the vastness of the domain.

Think of it, my brother Baines over there, pastor of El Paso, must come east or go south something like 500 miles to meet a brother pastor. Far down on the southren *[sic]* coast, on a narrow bank of sand, lashed by the waves of the Gulf, and "once the home of pirate Lafitte and his bloody crew," there is the city of Galveston. My brother Spalding is there. Then, way up yonder jutting into the Indian Territory is a cowboy pastor. They can visit each other about as well here at Richmond as at home. While here, on the far eastern border is Texarkana, where Texas fades into Arkansas and Louisiana. Bro. Cason, there, can only see Bro. Baines at El Paso by fath *[sic]*, not sight. They meet occasionally at the Southern Baptist Convention. Let me repeat again — you do not know us, you do not understand our affairs. The secretary of your Home Board, our good brother Tichenor, knows the field. He has been among us. His name is a household word among us.

With the out-spread map of Texas before us we have studied with him that great field and its necessities and possibities *[sic]*. His personal observations will confirm my statements. Our good brother, J. William Jones, can also bear testimony. Though he is no feather weight, he took such a flying trip across our territory as enables him to qualify as a witness.

But if you do not know us, we know you at least historically. The names of Broaddus, Jeter, Witt, Bagby, Poindexter, and the fiery Kerr with his "Dover Decrees" are all registered on our tablets, ineffaceable by time or change.

7th. My final argument is that what you do now will be like "bread cast upon the waters," returning to you in a few days. Outside of the reflex influence, it will yet yield you a hundred fold. The time is not distant when Texas shall rise like a young giant shaking himself before he goes out to self-sustaining independence. When the receiver shall become the benefactor. Who can say that in the approaching future, when your soil is worn out, your vitality expended, you will not cry out like the virgins in the parable, "Our lamps are going out; give us of your oil."

Should that time come it may be that some grateful Texan hand will rekindle the fires of your altars. You can all recall — the story is well told by Cooper and Irving — how the ancient Knickerbockers apparently buried their capital, by investment, in the wild lands of western New York. It was in the third generation before the profits accrued. But when they began to flow, they soon swelled into a flood of princely fortune. We must learn "to labor and to wait."

Allow me before I take my seat to emphasize certain great principles. When a tree stops growing it begins to die. When water stops flowing it stagnates, and stagnation is miasma and death. The best way to defend Rome is to carry the war into Africa. Aggression is true defence. The battles that defend our homes should be fought on the frontier and not around our firesides. Allow a homely illustration. The farmer who does not move his fence out must move it in. Thorns, briers *[sic]* and shrubs come up in the fence corners and invade the outside furrows. Contiguous trees overshadow the land just inside the fence. While coons, squirrels and other vermin harboring in their boughs come over the fence by night and day, making inroads on the growing crops. As you have noticed, the outside rows of corn are squirrel eaten. Now if the farmer yields to encroachment and moves in his fence the invasion follows and forces continued contraction until the very homestead is swallowed up. But what does a thrifty man do? He says, "I must preserve my clearing. To do that, I must deaden the timber outside, clean up the brush and keep moving my fence out, taking in the land lying next to me." So with the work of this Board. You cease to preserve what you have, when you cease to move your fences out. That man is preaching your funeral who says: "The work of this Board is about ended." It is life to you to push out into Florida. Be attracted by the everglades as much as the Beechers have been. Go where the ghost of the young Spaniard is yet searching for the fountain of youth and exorcise his illusion by showing that "a fountain has been opened in the house of David for sin and uncleanliness," and that "sinners plunged beneath that flood lose all their guilty stains." Carry the tidings into Louisiana. Make all her bayous baptismal witnesses of the resurrection. Push out your work into Arkansas. Push for your life as well as theirs. Study the great problems before you when you come up to these meetings.

Brethren, when God converted me from infidelity, he made me a missionary. My heart is in it. May that heart stop its beatings when it fails to love any man from any shore who is a child of God. I have, for illustration's sake, made some reference to the late civil war. It was not my purpose to revive any sectional feeling thereby. Palsied be my right hand when it fails to take in fraternal grasp the hand of any brother, though he once wore the blue. I have never been anywhere before. Never saw Mason's and Dickson's line until this trip. But was not surprised to see that the shores of the "bloody North" just over the Ohio were remarkably like the Southern shores. Their representatives here, bearing us friendly greetings, are much like our own brethren. We welcome them into this ship of life, bound with messages of salvation to every shore and to all people. In it I have embarked myself, my wife, my children, yea, all that I am and have, and hope to be asking the captain of my salvation to write his name on my brain, and on my hand, and on my heart, and all over me as a possession forever.

Endnotes

INTRODUCTION

1. Jeff D. Ray, *B. H. Carroll* (Nashville: Sunday School Board, 1927), 93, quoting J. B. Cranfill from unknown source.

CHAPTER 1

1. J. M. Carroll, "B. H. Carroll, D.D., LL.D.," in *Dr. B. H. Carroll, The Colossus of Baptist History*, comp. and ed. J. W. Crowder (Fort Worth: by the author, 1946), 14.

2. Ray, *Carroll*, 13; J. M. Carroll, "B. H. Carroll," 16. Ray and Carroll do not agree on the date of the move to Arkansas. Ray states that it occurred in 1847 when B. H. was four while Carroll states that the move occurred in 1850 or 1851 when B. H. was seven.

3. J. M. Carroll, "The Story of My Life, Chapters One Through Sixteen," *Journal of Texas Baptist History* 6 (1986): 75.

4. File 132, B. H. Carroll Collection, Archives, A. Webb Roberts Library, Southwestern Baptist Theological Seminary, Fort Worth (hereafter referred to as Carroll Collection); J. M. Carroll, "B. H. Carroll," 16–17.

5. J. M. Carroll, "B. H. Carroll," 18.

6. *Ibid.*

7. File 132, Carroll Collection. J. M. was the family historian; however, the majority of his work does not begin until the 1890s. A small book on the Carroll family history is located in File 151, J. M. Carroll Collection, Archives, A. Webb Roberts Library, Southwestern Baptist Theological Seminary, Fort Worth (hereafter referred to as J. M. Carroll Collection).

8. J. M. Carroll, "B. H. Carroll," 14–15; J. M. Carroll, "My Life," 37.

9. J. B. Cranfill, *B. H. Carroll and His Books* (Nashville: Broadman Press, n.d.), 5. Some confusion has arisen as to the spelling of Mary Eliza's maiden name. In J. M. Carroll's book *Dr. B. H. Carroll*, her name appears as Mallad; however, in J. M.'s handwritten notes her name appears as Mallard. See File 132, Carroll Collection.

10. File 132, Carroll Collection.

11. *Ibid.*

12. *Ibid.*

13. J. M. Carroll, "My Life," 18.

14. *Minute Book 1*, First Baptist Church, Caldwell, Tex., 7. The church later changed its name to First Baptist Church.

15. *Minutes of the Little River Association of Baptists*, 1859, 1.

16. *Ibid.*, 1860, 1.

17. *Ibid.*, 10.

18. *Ibid.*, 4.

19. J. M. Carroll, "B. H. Carroll," 13.

20. *Minutes of Little River*, 1861, 5–6.

21. J. M. Carroll, "B. H. Carroll," 14–15; File 132, Carroll Collection.

22. File 157, Carroll Collection.

23. *Ibid.*

24. *Ibid.*

25. *Ibid.*

26. *Ibid.*

27. *Ibid.*

28. *Ibid.* In later years B. H. indicated that voluntary withdrawal was not a valid way to leave the Baptist church. In a letter to E. C. Dragan dated November 24, 1908, on the subject of church membership, Carroll wrote: "there are but three ways of getting out of a Baptist church, first, by death, second by letter, and third by exclusion" (Box 4-1, Correspondence A–D, 1907–1910, E. C. Dragan Papers, Southern Baptist Archives and Library, Nashville, Tennessee).

29. File 157, Carroll Collection.

30. J. M. Carroll, "B. H. Carroll," 20.

31. Robert A. Baker, *Tell the Generations Following* (Nashville: Broadman Press, 1983), 57; J. M. Carroll, "B. H. Carroll," 23.

32. Ray, *Carroll*, 15; J. M. Carroll, "B. H. Carroll," 23.

33. J. M. Carroll, "B. H. Carroll," 22. Some question exists as to whether or not Carroll received a degree. Jeff D. Ray believes that Baylor granted Carroll a degree in 1861. Ray, *Carroll*, 15. W. W. Barnes states that Waco University granted Carroll an A.B. degree in 1861, making Carroll one of the senior men who followed Rufus Burleson to Waco. Baptist Biography File, Archives, A. Webb Roberts Library, Southwestern Baptist Theological Seminary, Fort Worth. The Alumni Directory of 1911, however, does not list Carroll as a graduate. He is listed in the 1920 directory as having received an honorary M.A. degree in 1871; yet there is no mention of his having obtained an earlier degree in the records of either Baylor University or Waco University.

34. J. M. Carroll, *A History of Texas Baptists*, ed. J. B. Cranfill (Dallas: Baptist Standard Publishing Co., 1923), 242.

35. J. M. Carroll, "B. H. Carroll," 40.

36. *Ibid.*, 41; J. M. Carroll, *History*, 242. A humorous sidelight to this story is in the two ways that J. M. records it. In one version he notes that Carroll was "never a great shot." In the other he states that Carroll "while a reasonably good marksman, was not in the class with his brother, J. M. Carroll."

37. Ray, *Carroll*, 16.

38. M. V. Smith, "B. H. Carroll, Pastor of First Baptist Church, Waco," *Texas Baptist Herald*, 25 July 1878, 2. The marriage license was issued to Carroll and O[phelia] Crunk, daughter of Nicolas S. Crunk on December 11, 1861. See Burleson County Marriage Records, iii, 73.

39. Smith, "Carroll," 2.

40. *Ibid.*; Civil Minutes of Burleson County, Book C, 277. A copy of the divorce decree can be found in File 157, Carroll Collection.

41. Burleson County Marriage Records, iii, 100.

42. File 157, Carroll Collection.

43. J. M. Carroll, "B. H. Carroll," 45.

44. James M. McPherson, *Battle Cry of Freedom* (New York: Oxford University Press, 1988), 602.

45. *Ibid.*, 614.

46. William W. Bennett, *A Narrative of the Great Revival* (Philadelphia: Claxton, Remsen, & Haffelfinger, 1877), 18. During his time in the army, Carroll apparently began to use tobacco, a habit that he would have for the rest of his life. Baker, *Generations*, 60.

47. File 157, Carroll Collection.

48. *Ibid.*

49. J. M. Carroll, "B. H. Carroll," 49–50.

50. J. M. Carroll, "B. H. Carroll," 55. Herman Norton notes that one problem for the Confederacy was the "low-caliber of chaplains" who ministered to some troops. *Rebel Religion* (St. Louis: Bethany Press, n.d.), 42. Chaplains such as these were no doubt easy prey for Carroll.

51. File 157, Carroll Collection.

52. J. M. Carroll, "B. H. Carroll," 45.

53. *Ibid.*, 47. The danger of injury or death by friendly fire for those who led charges into breastworks was high.

54. J. M. Carroll, "B. H. Carroll," 48. For a brief overview of the Battle of Mansfield, see Frances Kennedy, ed., *The Civil War Battlefield Guide* (Boston: Houghton Mifflin Co., 1990), 167–169.

55. J. M. Carroll, "B. H. Carroll," 48.

56. File 132, Carroll Collection.

57. For a complete text of the prayer see File 161, Carroll Collection.

58. File 157, Carroll Collection.

59. *Ibid.*

60. *Ibid.* A painting depicting this camp meeting hung for many years in the Tidwell Bible Building at Baylor University until it was stolen in the early 1980s.

61. File 132, Carroll Collection.

62. File 157, Carroll Collection.

63. Baker, *Generations*, 63.

CHAPTER 2

1. File 157, Carroll Collection; File 158, Carroll Collection. File 158 is listed as containing the personal notebook of B. H. Carroll. This author believes, however, that the notebook actually belonged to J. M. Carroll, who used it to record research for his biography on his brother.

2. *History First Baptist Church Caldwell, Texas*, Church History File 12, Ar-

chives, A. Webb Roberts Library, Southwestern Baptist Theological Seminary, Fort Worth; File 165, Carroll Collection.

3. J. M. Carroll, "B. H. Carroll," 72.

4. *Ibid.,* 69.

5. Ray, *Carroll,* 44.

6. *Ibid.,* 43.

7. *Ibid.,* 46.

8. Ironically, O'Bryan died of black jaundice and not yellow fever. *Ibid.,* 75.

9. File 158, Carroll Collection.

10. J. M. Carroll, "B. H. Carroll," 84.

11. *Ibid.,* 85.

12. File 165, Carroll Collection.

13. With a membership of fifty, New Hope was never a large church. It ceased to exist in 1885. J. L. Walker and C. P. Lumpkin, *History of the Waco Baptist Association of Texas* (Waco, Tex.: Byrne-Hill Printing House, 1897), 376.

14. Frank E. Burkhalter, *A World-Visioned Church* (Nashville: Broadman Press, 1946), 30.

15. First Baptist Church, Minute Book A, Meetings from May 31, 1851, to May 31, 1852, 1.

16. "First Baptist Church Celebrating 125 Years," *Waco Tribune-Herald,* 2 May 1976, sec. 3, p. 1.

17. Burkhalter, 44.

18. Walter Prescott Webb, ed. *Handbook of Texas* (Austin: Texas State Historical Association, 1952), s.v. "Waco, Texas," by Roger N. Conger; Dayton Kelley, ed., *Handbook of Waco and McLennan County, Texas* (Waco, Tex.: Texian Press, 1972), s.v. "Baptists in McLennan County."

19. John Sleeper and J. C. Hutchins, comps., *Waco and McLennan County, Texas* (repr., Waco, Tex.: Texian Press, 1966), 49.

20. FBC, Minute Book C, 225. Though some historians have stated that Carroll served as co-pastor at this time, the church minutes clearly show that he was, in fact, the assistant pastor to Burleson rather than his equal.

21. *Ibid.,* 242–245.

22. J. M. Carroll, "B. H. Carroll," 65–66.

23. Z. N. Morrell, *Flowers and Fruits in the Wilderness or Forty Six Years in Texas* (St. Louis: Commercial Printing Co., 1892), 363.

24. Ray, *Carroll,* 68.

25. J. M. Dawson, "Founder's Day Address," *Southwestern Evangel,* April 1927, 270, Archives, A. Webb Roberts Library, Southwestern Baptist Theological Seminary, Fort Worth.

26. *Texas Baptist Herald,* 10 May 1871, 2; *Ibid.,* 7 June 1871, 2.

27. File 165, Carroll Collection.

28. The guidelines for the debate can be found in the Carroll Collection, File 165.

29. J. M. Carroll, "Carroll," 143.

30. *Ibid.,* 145.

31. "Pen Pictures of Men of the General Association," *Texas Baptist,* 23 August 1877, 4.

32. FBC Minute Book C, 275.

33. File 31, Carroll Collection.

34. *Ibid.*

35. FBC Minute Book C, 378.

36. B. H. Carroll, "Baptist Church Polity and Articles of Faith," comp. J. W. Crowder, TMs, July 1957, A. Webb Roberts Library, Southwestern Baptist Theological Seminary, Fort Worth, 78.

37. *Ibid.,* 79–80. Despite Carroll's reluctance to ordain women, he was willing to give them the official title of "deaconess," a willingness which would put him at odds with many prominent Southern Baptist pastors today.

38. Burkhalter, 86.

39. FBC Minute Book C, 355–367.

40. Baker, *Generations*, 69, citing *Texas Baptist Herald.*

41. FBC Minute Book C, 369.

42. J. M. Carroll, *A History of Texas Baptists*, ed. J. B. Cranfill (Dallas: Baptist Standard Publishing Co., 1923), 496; FBC Minute Book C, 391.

43. Tension between Carroll and the church appeared as early as 1873 when, by a vote of fifteen to twelve, the church passed a motion that stated "our pastor ought to occupy in person our pulpit at our stated times of preaching." Carroll was away from the church too often for many members. The closeness of the vote shows how divisive the issue must have been. The problem is never mentioned again, however, indicating that it must have been resolved. FBC Minute Book C, 275.

44. FBC Minute Book C, 391–398.

45. *Ibid.,* 398.

46. Burkhalter, 124–125.

47. FBC Minute Book C, 333, citing the committee's resolutions. The resolutions may also be found in File 663, Carroll Collection.

48. FBC Minute Book C, 334.

49. B. H. Carroll, "The Temperance Question," *Texas Baptist Herald*, 8 June 1874, 1.

50. File 644, Carroll Collection.

51. J. M. Carroll, *History*, 409.

52. Ray, *Carroll*, 134.

53. For a more detailed account see J. M. Carroll, *History*, 422–427; Rufus C. Burleson, *The Life and Writings of Rufus C. Burleson*, comp. Georgia Burleson (n.p., 1901), 442–446; "The Education Commission," *Texas Baptist Herald*, 8 November 1877, 1.

54. *Minutes of the Waco Baptist Association*, 1871, 5.

55. Walker and Lumpkin, 67, citing *Minutes of WBA*, 1874.

56. *Minutes of the General Baptist Association*, 1871, 7.

57. *Ibid.,* 1875, 6, 9; 1878, 16–17; 1879, 9, 26.

58. *Ibid.,* 1877, 35; 1880, 13, 21.

59. B. H. Carroll, "Controversies," comp. J. W. Crowder, TMs, 12 July 1940, A. Webb Roberts Library, Southwestern Baptist Theological Seminary, Fort Worth, 1.

60. *Ibid.,* 4. For more information on this controversy see *Texas Baptist Herald*, 4 February 1875, 1; 3 June 1875, 1; 10 June 1875, 1.

61. One wonders what Carroll's attitude would be today with the increasing

emphasis on bivocational ministers in pioneer areas.

62. J. B. Link, "The Overton Convention," *Texas Baptist Herald*, 20 December 1877.

63. B. H. Carroll, "The Overton Convention," *Texas Baptist Herald*, 17 January 1878.

64. For further information on the controversy between Carroll and Link, see *Texas Baptist Herald*, 17 January 1877 through 7 February 1878.

65. Keith Cogburn, "B. H. Carroll and Controversy: A Study of His Leadership Among Texas Baptists, 1871–1899" (M.A. thesis, Baylor University, 1983), 34.

66. J. M. Carroll, "B. H. Carroll," 133.

67. File 723, Carroll Collection.

68. M. V. Smith, "Correspondence," *Texas Baptist Herald*, 25 July 1878, 2.

69. *Ibid.* Carroll's divorce came to haunt him once again in 1890, when rumors concerning it flared. At that time Carroll believed that S. A. Hayden was circulating the rumors, a charge that Hayden denied.

70. FBC Minute Book D, 11–12. For more information on the Southern Baptist Convention's annual meeting in Waco, see *Waco Examiner*, 8 May 1883, 3; 9 May 1883, 4; 10 May 1883, 4.

CHAPTER 3

1. John R. Sampey, Louisville, Kentucky, to B. H. Carroll, Waco, Texas, ALS, 24 August 1896, File 208–1, Carroll Collection.

2. B. H. Carroll, "A Sermon to Preachers," *Guardian* 11 (November 1892): 575.

3. *Ibid.*, 576.

4. *Ibid.*

5. *Ibid.*, 577. Carroll's report of this young man's ministry would seem to describe the ministry of many Southern Baptist pastors today.

6. B. H. Carroll, "Memorials, Meetings And Miscellanies," comp. J. W. Crowder, TMs [carbon copy], A. Webb Roberts Library, Southwestern Baptist Theological Seminary, Fort Worth, 172.

7. Charles B. Williams, "B. H. Carroll: The Titanic Interpreter and Teacher of Truth," TMs, A. Webb Roberts Library, Southwestern Baptist Theological Seminary, Fort Worth, 20. This work is an invaluable resource in studying Carroll, as Williams writes from the viewpoint of both student and colleague. The work, however, is far from objective. In recalling Carroll's life, Williams compares him to many of the great figures in history including Paul, Napoleon, Helen Keller, and Franklin D. Roosevelt.

8. Ray, *Carroll*, 68.

9. S. P. Brooks, "B. H. Carroll and Baylor University," in *Dr. B. H. Carroll: The Colossus of Baptist History*, comp. and ed. J. W. Crowder (Fort Worth: by the author, 1946), 123.

10. Williams, 20.

11. J. M. Carroll, "B. H. Carroll," 28. While Carroll was a teacher, he taught many of his students this method.

12. Many of the books that were in Carroll's library at the time of his death are now located in A. Webb Roberts Library, Southwestern Baptist Theological Seminary, Fort Worth.

13. J. M. Carroll, "B. H. Carroll," 25.

14. Williams, 27.

15. Carroll's sermons can be found in a number of books. See the bibliography for specific references.

16. B. H. Carroll, *Christ and His Church*, comp. J. W. Crowder (Dallas: Helms Printing Co., 1940), 135–168.

17. B. H. Carroll, *The Agnostic: A Sermon* (Gatesville, Tex.: "Advance" Book and Job Printing Establishment, 1884), 16.

18. B. H. Carroll, "Cold Water," *Waco Daily Examiner*, 13 August 1885, 4.

19. "Repression," *Waco Daily Examiner*, 15 August 1885, 4.

20. B. H. Carroll, "Roger Q. Mills," *Galveston Daily News*, 12 August 1885, 5.

21. B. H. Carroll, "Whiskey Traffic," *Galveston Daily News*, 20 August 1885, 5.

22. J. M. Teague wrote to Carroll stating: "I have read your sermon on prohibition in the 'News'. . . and am anxious for you to write me a rousing speech upon the question" (J. M. Teague, Longview, to B. H. Carroll, Waco, ALS, 24 August 1885, File 644, Carroll Collection). W. W. Moore of Stephenville noted that as the election approached, the Stephenville paper refused to print Carroll's speeches, carrying only the comments of Coke. W. W. Moore, Stephenville, to B. H. Carroll, Waco, ALS, 23 August 1885, File 644, Carroll Collection.

23. "Captain Elgin on Prohibition," *Galveston Daily News*, 26 August 1885, 5; "Prohibition vs. Democracy," *Waco Daily Examiner*, 21 August 1885, 2; "The Church and Prohibition," *Waco Daily Examiner*, 29 August 1885, 2.

24. "The Barbecue," *Waco Day*, 29 August 1885, 1.

25. "The Anti-prohibitionists," *Galveston Daily News*, 30 August 1885, 1.

26. Richard Coke, Waco, to B. H. Carroll, Waco, TLS, 25 February 1886, File 226, Carroll Collection.

27. B. H. Carroll, "Carroll's Reply to Coke," *Texas Baptist Herald*, 10 September 1885, 1.

28. *Ibid.*

29. "Texas Press Opinion," *Waco Day*, 2 September 1885, 1.

30. Thomas J. Brian, "The 1887 Prohibition Crusade in Texas" (M.A. thesis, Baylor University, 1972), 5–13.

31. "An Earnest Appeal to All Prohibitionists," *Waco Advance*, 3 March 1887, 1; "Closing Scenes," *Waco Day*, 16 March 1887, 1.

32. B. H. Carroll, "Patriotism and Prohibition," comp. J. W. Crowder, TMs, 1951, A. Webb Roberts Library, Southwestern Baptist Theological Seminary, Fort Worth, 98.

33. *Ibid.*, see full collection of articles for further examples of Carroll's arguments concerning personal liberty.

34. "Carroll's Modes," *Waco Daily Examiner*, 10 June 1887, 31; "A Matter of Leadership," *Waco Daily Examiner*, 18 May 1887, 4.

35. George W. McDaniel, *A Memorial Wreath* (n.p., n.d.), 19.

36. Ray, *Carroll*, 122–123.

37. In "Prohibition Campaign," *Dallas Morning News*, 7 July 1887, 5, the reporter stated that the debate influenced no more than fifty votes.

38. File 267, Carroll Collection.

39. The possibility remains that Carroll actually did write the grocer's note produced by Mills, but he was so shocked by the development that he was forced

to deny it. Mills never admitted that the note was a forgery but only that Carroll denied writing it.

40. *Minutes of WBA*, 1888, 3–4.

41. Walker and Lumpkin, 267–268.

42. J. M. Carroll, *History*, 639.

43. *Minutes of BGA*, 1883, 19, citing the committee's report.

44. *Ibid.*, 1883, 20.

45. *Ibid.*, 1884, 17, citing Carroll's report.

46. *Ibid.*, 1885, 13–18; *Minutes of the Baptist State Convention*, 1885, 12.

47. J. M. Carroll, *History*, 649.

48. *Ibid.*, citing the subcommittee's recommendation. According to J. B. Cranfill, J.M. Carroll, not the subcommittee, developed the plan for consolidation. See footnote on p. 651.

49. *Proceedings of the Baptist General Convention of Texas*, 1886, 24. Before the vote was taken, R. T. Hanks warned the convention against involving itself in personal matters.

50. *Proceedings of BGCT*, 1886, 24; J. M. Carroll, *History*, 658–659.

51. B. H. Carroll, "Our Texas Schools and Christian Education," comp. J. W. Crowder, TMs, A. Webb Roberts Library, Southwestern Baptist Theological Seminary, Fort Worth, 49.

52. *Ibid.*

53. FBC Minute Book D, 239.

54. George W. Truett, Dallas, to B. H. Carroll, Waco, ALS, 20 May 1891, File 101, Carroll Collection.

55. Powhatan W. James, *George W. Truett: A Biography* (Nashville: Broadman Press, 1939), 63–65.

56. Carroll did not confine his fundraising efforts to Texas. See John D. Rockefeller, New York, to B. H. Carroll, Waco, Tex., ALS, 16 May 1892, File 99, Carroll Collection.

57. *Ibid.*, 77.

58. *Proceedings of BGCT*, 1895, 50–51. For more information on Brann see Charles Carver, *Brann and the Iconoclast* (Austin: University of Texas Press, 1957).

59. Cogburn, 113–114.

60. Though both the Brann and Hayden controversies caused tension between Burleson and Carroll, the tension may have developed much earlier. In a letter from Burleson to Carroll dated March 5, 1891, Burleson was clearly on the defensive in explaining his disciplinary actions against Carroll's son B. H., Jr. File 168, Carroll Collection.

61. Burleson, 464, citing the board's substitute motion.

62. *Ibid.*, 464–465.

63. See *Texas Baptist and Herald*, June–August 1897.

64. The full statement is located in File 119, Carroll Collection.

65. M. S. Pierson, n.p., to B. H. Carroll, Waco, ALS, 9 September 1897, File 93, Carroll Collection.

66. Ray, *Carroll*, 97–98.

67. Baker, *Generations*, 87.

68. File 8, Carroll Collection. The address is in Carroll's own handwriting.

69. *Ibid.*

70. File 75, Carroll Collection.

71. *Ibid.*

72. Ray, *Carroll*, 100; also see Williams, 118.

73. File 269, Carroll Collection.

74. M. T. Martin, *Theological and Doctrinal Views of M. T. Martin as Found in His Editorials in the Gospel Standard and Standard Expositor* (Atlanta: Gress and Sexton, n.d.), 9.

75. "General Hawthorne's Conversion and Points of Doctrine Involved," *Texas Baptist Herald*, 26 February 1885, 1; "Ordination of Bro. A. T. Hawthorne," *Texas Baptist Herald*, 9 April 1988, 2.

76. Martin, *Views*, 4.

77. "Editorial," *Texas Baptist Herald*, 29 August 1888, 4.

78. M. T. Martin, "Motive and Aims," *The Gospel Standard*, January 1888, quoted in *Trial of M. T. Martin by First Baptist Church at Waco, Texas* (Waco, Tex.: Press of Kellner Steam Printing Co., 1889), 16, File 595, Carroll Collection.

79. "Rev. M. T. Martin's Doctrine Endorsed," *Texas Baptist and Herald*, 13 February 1889, 4.

80. A. J. Holt, Dallas, to B. H. Carroll, Waco, TL, 28 January 1889, File 590, Carroll Collection.

81. B. H. Carroll, "Bro. Carroll Reviews Bro. Martin," *Texas Baptist and Herald*, 13 February 1889, 4.

82. M. T. Martin, "Response to Bro. Carroll's Review," *Texas Baptist and Herald*, 27 February 1889, 4.

83. *Ibid.*

84. B. H. Carroll, "From Bro. Carroll," *Texas Baptist and Herald*, 6 March 1889, 4; *Ibid.,* 20 March 1889, 1.

85. B. H. Carroll and Rufus C. Burleson, Waco, to [Texas Baptist pastors], TL, 22 March 1889, File 590, Carroll Collection.

86. File 593, Carroll Collection.

87. *Ibid.*

88. *Ibid.*

89. File 590, Carroll Collection.

90. H. H. Tucker, Atlanta, Georgia, to B. H. Carroll, Waco, Texas, ALS, 12 August 1889.

91. "Report Adopted by the Waco Church," *Texas Baptist and Herald*, 29 January 1890, 6.

92. For a complete report on the Waco-Marlin conflict, see Walker and Lumpkin, 143–147, 159–160.

93. Files 590–592, Carroll Collection.

94. Walker and Lumpkin, 195–196; J. M. Carroll, *History*, 723.

95. Presnall H. Wood and Floyd W. Thatcher, *Prophets with Pens: A History of the Baptist Standard* (Dallas: Baptist Standard Publishing Co., 1969), 13–14.

96. B. H. Carroll, "The Paper Question," *Texas Baptist and Herald*, 20 November 1890, 1.

97. "Dr. B. H. Carroll on the Paper Question," *Western Baptist*, 27 November 1890, 1.

98. S. A. Hayden, Dallas, to B. H. Carroll, Waco, TLS, 5 July 1890, File 168,

Carroll Collection.

99. B. H. Carroll, Waco, to S. A. Hayden, Dallas, ALS, 5 December 1893; 12 January 1894, File 252, Carroll Collection.

100. "Dr. Carroll's Sermons," *Texas Baptist and Herald*, 11 January 1894, 4; "Our Reply," *Texas Baptist and Herald*, 18 January 1894, 4.

101. J. M. Carroll, *History*, 708.

102. J. M. Carroll, Waco, to S. A. Hayden, Dallas, ALS, 22 May 1894; S. A. Hayden, Dallas, to J. M. Carroll, Waco, TLS, 26 May 1894, File 179, J. M. Carroll Collection.

103. J. M. Carroll, *History*, 710–711, citing Carroll's resolution.

104. Robert A. Baker, *The Southern Baptist Convention and Its People: 1607–1972* (Nashville: Broadman Press, 1974), 278–280.

105. J. M. Carroll, *History*, 717.

106. *Ibid.*, 718, citing the board's report.

107. S. A. Hayden, "Centralization," *Texas Baptist and Herald*, 23 January 1896, 5.

108. B. H. Carroll, "Cooperation," *Baptist Standard*, 12 March 1896, 6.

109. "Will Not Meet at Weatherford," *Texas Baptist and Herald*, 26 August 1897, 1. In an effort to convince Weatherford, a stronghold of Hayden supporters, to hold the convention, Hayden offered the church $1,200 and the use of 100 tents and 800 cots.

110. File 173, Carroll Collection.

111. E. E. Gibson, *The Hayden-Cranfill Conspiracy Trial* (Dallas: Baptist Publishing Co., 1900), 29.

112. J. M. Carroll, *History*, 801–804.

113. *Proceedings of BGCT*, 1898, 11–24; 1899, 17; 1900, 13.

114. For Hayden's account of the controversy see S. A. Hayden, *The Complete Conspiracy Trial Book* (Dallas: Texas Baptist Publishing House, 1907). At one point during the latter stages of the controversy, Hayden accused Carroll of planning his murder. S. A. Hayden, "Report," *Texas Baptist and Herald*, 24 August 1899, 9.

115. A concise overview of Carroll's theology can be found in James Spivey, "Theology of B. H. Carroll," unpublished paper, 1990, Southwestern Baptist Theological Seminary, Fort Worth.

116. B. H. Carroll, "Church Polity," 38.

117. B. H. Carroll, *Inspiration of the Bible*, ed., J. B. Cranfill (New York: F. H. Revell Co., 1930), 49.

118. B. H. Carroll, "Church Polity," 4.

119. Baker, *Generations*, 80.

120. B. H. Carroll, "Church Polity," 11.

121. J. R. Graves, *Old Landmarkism: What is It?*, 2d ed. (Texarkana, Tex.: Baptist Sunday School Committee, 1928), 33.

122. Wilson Lanning Stewart, "Ecclesia: The Motif of B. H. Carroll's Theology" (Th.D. thesis, Southwestern Baptist Theological Seminary, 1959), 37.

123. File 583, Carroll Collection; J. R. Graves, *The Work of Christ Consummated in Seven Dispensations* (Memphis: J. R. Graves & Sons, 1883), 255.

124. Graves, *Landmarkism*, 122.

125. J. R. Graves, "Editorial," *Tennessee Baptist*, 5 February 1859, 2.

126. *Minutes of WBA*, 1884, statistical tables; 1898, 27.

127. File 567, J. M. Carroll Collection.

128. FBC Minute Book C, 20 February 1887.

129. *Ibid.*, 6 March 1887.

130. *Ibid.*, October 1895.

131. Burkhalter, 127–128, citing Judge Jenkins (clerk).

132. *Ibid.*, 131.

133. B. H. Carroll, Waco, Texas, to T.T. Eaton, Louisville, Kentucky, ALS, 15 January 1898, T. T. Eaton Papers, Southern Baptist Convention Archives, Nashville, Tennessee.

134. File 14, Carroll Collection; Burkhalter, 135.

CHAPTER 4

1. Baker, *Generations*, 65, citing *Texas Baptist Herald*, 16 January 1867. This article can also be found in File 18, Carroll Collection.

2. Baker, *Generations*, 67; J. M. Carroll, "B. H. Carroll," 86.

3. J. M. Carroll, *History*, 412. Carroll noted in speaking of these addresses that "one [was] before the Philomathesian Society on 'The Good and True Orator,' the other before the young ladies of the Philomathesian Society on 'The Current Literature of the Day — Its Tendency upon the Character and Position of Women.'" These addresses are located in Files 2–3, Carroll Collection.

4. *Minutes of WBA*, 1871, 5.

5. Helen Bagby Harrison, *The Bagbys of Brazil* (Crawford, Tex.: Crawford Christian Press, n.d.), 3.

6. Ray, *Carroll*, 134.

7. Prince E. Burroughs, "Founder's Day Address," delivered at Southwestern Baptist Theological Seminary, Fort Worth, Texas, 14 March 1935, Archives, A. Webb Roberts Library, Southwestern Baptist Theological Seminary, Fort Worth.

8. *Proceedings of BGCT*, 1886, 21–25.

9. Burkhalter, 133.

10. *Proceedings of BGCT*, 1890, 35.

11. *Ibid.*, 1893, 81–82.

12. *Ibid.*, 1894, 60–61.

13. *Ibid.*, 1895, 59. Carroll was reelected yearly with the regular faculty; Baylor University (Waco, Texas), Minutes of the Meetings of the Board of Trustees, 1895–1905, 20.

14. John S. Tanner, Louisville, Kentucky, to B. H. Carroll, Waco, Texas, TLS, 1895, File 171, Carroll Collection.

15. *Proceedings*, BGCT, 1898, 48.

16. Baker, *Generations*, 99.

17. *Ibid.*, 102, citing W. T. Conner, source unknown.

18. W. O. Carver, "William Heth Whitsitt: The Seminary's First Martyr," *Review and Expositor* 51 (October 1954): 449. For more on the life of Whitsitt see E. B. Pollard, "The Life and Work of William Heth Whitsitt," *Review and Expositor* 9 (April 1912): 159–184; Rufus W. Weaver, "The Life and Times of William Heth Whitsitt," *Review and Expositor* 37 (April 1940): 113–122.

19. William H. Whitsitt, *A Question in Baptist History* (Louisville: Charles Dearing, 1896), 15; Pollard, 175; Carver, 457.

20. Pollard, 173. These editorials were reprinted in the *Baptist Standard*, 11 and 18 June 1896, 4. Though Whitsitt claimed that this was his first statement concerning Baptists and baptism, James Tull believes that there was an "intriguing possibility" that Whitsitt might have been the author of a sting attack on Landmarkism published under the pseudonym "Pike" that appeared in *(Richmond) Religious Herald*, 23 March 1876, 1. In this article Pike stated that Baptists rediscovered immersion in 1640. James E. Tull, "A Study of Southern Baptist Landmarkism in the Light of Historical Baptist Ecclesiology," 2 vols. (Ph.D. diss., Columbia University, 1960), 2:580–581.

21. William Heth Whitsitt, Louisville, Kentucky, to B. H. Carroll, Waco, Texas, TLS, 18 December 1894, File 208–1, Carroll Collection.

22. See Carroll's letter, *Baptist Standard*, 7 May 1896, 13.

23. *Southern Baptist Convention Annual*, 1896, 28–29; Cogburn, 81.

24. A. R. Miller, Bonham, to B. H. Carroll, Waco, ALS, 12 June 1896, File 208–1, Carroll Collection. Miller continued: "Why if some backwoods preacher, but little knowing, and of very little influence, were to commit such an offence he would be arraigned before the church, and due satisfaction would have to be given or he would be expelled from his church" *(Ibid.)*.

25. A. R. Miller, Bonham, to B. H. Carroll, Waco, ALS, July 1896, File 208–1, Carroll Collection.

26. A. T. Robertson, Louisville, Kentucky, to B. H. Carroll, Waco, Texas, ALS, 15 July 1896, File 208–1, Carroll Collection. Apparently this was not the first time that Robertson had written to Carroll about Whitsitt, for he closed his letter by stating: "I beg pardon for appealing to you a second time, but wisdom was never more needed among Southern Baptists."

27. John R. Sampey, Louisville, Kentucky, to B. H. Carroll, Waco, Texas, ALS, 24 August 1896, File 208–1, Carroll Collection.

28. *Proceedings of BGCT*, 1896, 68, citing Carroll's resolution.

29. B. H. Carroll, "The Whitsitt Case at Wilmington," *Baptist Standard*, 20 May 1897, 1. The address can also be found in File 208–1, Carroll Collection.

30. The Southern Baptist Theological Seminary (Louisville, Kentucky), Minutes of Meetings of the Board of Trustees, meeting of 6 May 1897, Book 2, 221–222, quoted in Baker, *Generations*, 92, n. 104.

31. B. H. Carroll, "Wilmington," 1.

32. William Heth Whitsitt, "Dr. Whitsitt's Address to the Students," delivered at Southern Baptist Theological Seminary, Louisville, Kentucky, May 1897, File 208–1, Carroll Collection. This address can also be found in *(Louisville) Western Recorder*, 27 May 1897, 5.

33. B. H. Carroll, "Back to the Realm of Discussion," *Baptist Standard*, 27 May 1897, 1. This article can also be found in File 60, Carroll Collection.

34. B. H. Carroll, "The Real Issue in the Whitsitt Case," *Baptist Standard*, 5 August 1897, 3.

35. *Ibid.*

36. *SBC Annual*, May 1898, 23, citing Carroll's motion.

37. William A. Mueller, *A History of Southern Baptist Theological Seminary* (Nashville: Broadman Press, 1959), 172.

38. Tull, 2:616.

39. *American Baptist Flag*, 6 October 1898, 4, File 208–1, Carroll Collection.

40. F. H. Kerfoot, Louisville, Kentucky, to B. H. Carroll, Waco, Texas, ALS, 4 April 1898, File 208–1, Carroll Collection.

41. Tull, 616.

42. A. T. Robertson, Louisville, Kentucky, to B. H. Carroll, Waco, Texas, ALS, 13 March 1911, File 208–1, Carroll Collection.

43. Ray, *Carroll*, 127.

44. J. M. Carroll, *History*, 835. Burroughs stated in his Founder's Day address that the board considered Carroll for the presidency of Baylor in 1899, but Carroll refused to allow the trustees to vote on his nomination. Although possibly accurate, Burroughs' account cannot be considered to be historically reliable. Burroughs stated that after Carroll declined a vote allowing his name to be considered, the trustees elected S. P. Brooks to the presidency. In 1899, however, the board actually elected Oscar H. Cooper to be president of Baylor. After Cooper's resignation in 1902, the board elected Brooks to the presidency.

45. Baker, *Generations*, 111.

46. File 14, Carroll Collection.

47. R. B. Morgan, Fort Worth, to B. H. Carroll, Waco, ALS, 2 May 1897, File 208–1, Carroll Collection.

48. Baylor, Minutes of Trustees, 21 March 1900, 140.

49. B. H. Carroll, "Theological Department at Baylor," *Baptist Standard*, 16 November 1905, W. W. Barnes Collection, Archives, A. Webb Roberts Library, Southwestern Baptist Theological Seminary, Fort Worth (hereafter referred to as Barnes Collection).

50. Considering Carroll's role in the Whitsitt Controversy, his ability to attract highly respected instructors to Baylor is noteworthy.

51. Carroll's salary at that time was fixed at $2,500, second only to the president's salary and $1,000 more than any other professor's at the university. Baylor, Minutes of Trustees, 1 January 1904.

52. Baylor, Minutes of Trustees, 31 August 1905. During Southwestern's formative years from 1901 to 1905, Carroll still served as president of the board of trustees at Baylor.

53. Baylor, Minutes of Trustees, 31 August 1905.

54. J. W. Bailey, "Editorial," *(Raleigh) Biblical Recorder*, 10 July 1901.

55. R. N. Barrett, *Baptist Standard*, 29 August 1901, 1.

56. Baker, *Generations*, 117.

57. *Proceedings of BGCT*, 1903, 44.

58. *Encyclopedia of Southern Baptists*, s.v. "Southwestern Baptist Theological Seminary," by W. W. Barnes.

59. B. H. Carroll, *(Raleigh) Biblical Recorder*, 25 March 1903, 3. The American Baptist Education Society had clear reservations about the Theological Department at Baylor; and as a result the society wondered whether it wanted to help found a new theological seminary, even indirectly, through its gifts. In his response to these concerns, Carroll stated that the funds for the Theological Department were separate from the rest of the school, avoiding the issue of the department's becoming a seminary. Correspondence on this issue reveals how Carroll presented the department to Baptists outside of the South. Unfortunately, the majority of the correspondence is lost. File 78, Carroll Collection.

60. Ray, *Carroll*, 136–138.

61. Baker, *Generations*, 121.

62. B. H. Carroll, "Opening Address Before the Theological Department Baylor University," *Baptist Standard*, 14 September 1905, 1, Barnes Collection.

63. J. W. Bailey, "Editorial," *(Raleigh) Biblical Recorder*, 27 September 1905, quoted in Baker, *Generations*, 124.

64. W. W. Barnes, *The Southern Baptist Convention, 1845–1953* (Nashville: Broadman Press, 1954), 202.

65. This chair, commonly called "the chair of fire," became the first endowed chair at the seminary. *Proceedings of BGCT*, 1906, 42–51.

66. *Ibid.*, 44. In making this statement, Carroll failed to recognize the years of work that he and others had given to making this "beginning" successful. In many ways the seminary's opening was not a beginning at all but rather a continuation of the growth and development of an earlier work.

67. See the report from George W. Truett, *Ibid.*, 27; J. B. Gambrell, "Baylor University as an Educational Force," *Baptist Standard*, 2 November 1906, 1 ff.

68. *Proceedings of BGCT*, 1907, 52.

69. Baylor, Minutes of Trustees, 1906–1914, 27. The trustees named Carroll as chairman of this committee; others serving were Jeff D. Ray, W. H. Jenkins, and S. P. Brooks.

70. File 177, Carroll Collection.

71. S. P. Brooks, Shreveport, Louisiana, to B. H. Carroll, Waco, Texas, ALS, 26 June 1907, File 177, Carroll Collection.

72. *Ibid.*

73. Baker, *Generations*, 128.

74. Baylor, Minutes of Trustees, 1906–1914, 46–47.

75. *Proceedings of BGCT*, 1907, 45–46. Baker believes that Carroll wanted to move the entire ministerial education program at Baylor to the seminary. The committee's report ensured the continuation of ministerial training at Baylor (Baker, 132).

76. Baylor, Minutes of Trustees, 1907, 50.

77. Southwestern Baptist Theological Seminary (Fort Worth), Minutes of the Meetings of the Board of Trustees, 1907, 6.

78. *Ibid.*, 8–9.

79. B. H. Carroll, "Southwestern Baptist Theological Seminary," *Baptist Standard*, 26 March 1908, 1.

80. *Ibid.*; see also Baker, *Generations*, 137.

81. SWBTS, Minutes of Trustees, 8 May 1908, 17.

82. B. H. Carroll, "SWBTS," 1.

83. SWBTS, Minutes of Trustees, 12 November 1908, 21.

84. *Ibid.*, 22.

85. *Ibid.*

86. B. H. Carroll, "Southwestern Baptist Theological Seminary, Article Three," *Baptist Standard*, 2 April 1908, 1. For a more detailed discussion of the move to Fort Worth, see Baker, *Generations*, 145–160.

87. P. E. Burroughs, "Fort Worth Launches a Campaign to Secure Southwestern Baptist Theological Seminary," *Baptist Standard*, 9 April 1908, 1.

88. George W. Truett Collection, File 815, Archives, A. Webb Roberts Library, Southwestern Baptist Theological Seminary, Fort Worth.

89. R. C. Buckner, Dallas, to B. H. Carroll, Waco, ALS, File 177, Carroll Collection.

90. Files 178–179, Carroll Collection.

91. SWBTS, Minutes of Trustees, 21 September 1909, 27; "Fort Worth Gets Baptist Seminary," *Fort Worth Star-Telegram*, 22 September 1909, 12.

92. L. R. Scarborough, *A Modern School of the Prophets* (Nashville: Broadman Press, 1939), 64. In the weeks that followed, the *Star-Telegram* gave an almost daily update on the campaign's progress. See *Fort Worth Star-Telegram*, 25 September 1909 through 23 October 1909.

93. "Seminary Site South of City," *Fort Worth Star-Telegram*, 3 November 1909, 3–4.

94. SWBTS, Minutes of Trustees, 2 November 1909, 39.

95. Scarborough, 73.

96. J. M. Carroll, "B. H. Carroll," 119–120.

97. *Ibid.*, 120.

98. The Carroll Collection at Southwestern includes many of Carroll's lectures as well as his student exams and notebooks.

99. The bibliography of this work includes a full listing of Carroll's published works.

100. Baker, *Generations*, 165.

101. B. H. Carroll, Waco, to L. R. Scarborough, Abilene, TLS, 1 November 1906, Scarborough Papers, Archives, A. Webb Roberts Library, Southwestern Baptist Theological Seminary, Fort Worth.

102. SWBTS, Minutes of Trustees, May, 1913, 108–109.

103. J. Frank Norris, *Inside History of First Baptist Church, Fort Worth, and Temple Baptist Church, Detroit* (N.p., 1945), 127.

104. G. H. Connell, Fort Worth, to B. H. Carroll, Fort Worth, ALS, 5 October 1912, File 183, Carroll Collection.

105. B. H. Carroll, Fort Worth, to G. H. Connell, Fort Worth, TLS, 19 October 1912, File 183, Carroll Collection; Baker, *Generations*, 181.

106. H. Leon McBeth, "J. Frank Norris and Southwestern Baptist Theological Seminary," unpublished paper, 11–12, Southwestern Baptist Theological Seminary, Fort Worth.

107. Southwestern Baptist Theological Seminary (Fort Worth), Minutes of the Meetings of the Faculty, 1912; Baker, *Generations*, 166.

108. Baker, *Generations*, 166. These letters, thought to be lost, were recently discovered. Newman's resignation was in compliance with Carroll's request. Reeves' letter, however, left little doubt that his resignation was not voluntary. "Dear Sir: In accordance with your wishes I hereby tender my resignation" (SWBTS, Minutes of Trustees, 1914, inserted loose-leaf style in book).

109. File entitled "Life in Southwestern Seminary," Barnes Collection. Barnes went on to state, with some surprise, that Carroll never asked him for his view of Baptist church succession.

110. Baptist Biography File. Following Carroll's death Hallie returned to Waco, where she lived for a short time before moving to Los Angeles to join her son, Harrison. She died in 1938 at the age of seventy-seven.

111. George W. Truett, "Funeral Discourse," *Baptist Standard*, 19 November 1914, 4.

112. *Baptist Standard*, 3 December 1914, 4.
113. *Ibid.*
114. *Ibid.*
115. Carroll's influence was felt even in J. Frank Norris' independent Baptist seminary, as one of the courses offered there was "The English Bible." Carroll's name has continued to be tied to controversy in the late twentieth century as both sides of the Inerrancy Controversy within the Southern Baptist Convention quote from his works.

CHAPTER 5

1. Scarborough, 90.
2. Barnes, *Convention*, 209.

Selected Bibliography

PRIMARY SOURCES

Published Materials

Bailey, J. W. "Editorial." *(Raleigh) Biblical Recorder,* 10 July 1901.
————. "Editorial." *(Raleigh) Biblical Recorder,* 25 March 1903, 3.
Burleson, Rufus C. *The Life and Writings of Rufus C. Burleson.* Compiled by Georgia Burleson, N.p., 1901.
Burroughs, P. E. "Benajah Harvey Carroll." In *Ten Men From Baylor,* ed. J. M. Price, 63–78. Kansas City: Central Seminary Press, 1945.
Carroll, B. H. *The Acts.* Edited by J. B. Cranfill. Chicago: F. H. Revell Co., 1916.
————. *The Agnostic: A Sermon.* Gatesville, Texas: "Advance" Book and Job Printing Establishment, 1884.
————. *Ambitious Dreams of Youth.* Compiled by J. W. Crowder. Edited by J. B. Cranfill. Dallas: Helms Printing Co., 1939.
————. "Back to the Realm of Discussion." *Baptist Standard,* 27 May 1897, 1.
————. *Baptism.* Waco, Texas: Baptist Standard Press, 1893.
————. *Baptist Church Polity and Articles of Faith.* Compiled by J. W. Crowder. Fort Worth, 1957. Archives, A. Webb Roberts Library, Southwestern Baptist Theological Seminary, Fort Worth.
————. *Baptists and Their Doctrines.* Compiled by J. B. Cranfill. Chicago: F. H. Revell Co., 1913.
————. *Baylor University Historical Sketch.* Waco, Texas: Kellner Press, n.d.
————. *Bible Doctrine of Repentance.* N.p.: Baptist Book, 1897.
————. *The Book of Genesis.* Edited by J. B. Cranfill. Chicago: F. H. Revell Co., 1913.

————. *The Book of Revelation.* Edited by J. B. Cranfill. Chicago: F. H. Revell Co., 1913.

————. *The Books of Exodus and Leviticus.* Edited by J. B. Cranfill. Chicago: F. H. Revell Co., 1914.

————. *The Books of Numbers to Ruth.* Edited by J. B. Cranfill. Chicago: F. H. Revell Co., 1914.

————. *Christ and His Church.* Compiled by J. W. Crowder. Edited by J. B. Cranfill. Dallas: Helms Printing Co., 1940.

————. *Christian Education and Some Social Problems, Sermons.* Compiled and edited by J. W. Crowder. Fort Worth, 1948.

————. *Christ's Marching Orders.* Compiled by J. W. Crowder. Edited by J. B. Cranfill. Dallas: Helms Printing Co., 1941.

————. *Colossians, Ephesians, and Hebrews.* Edited by J. B. Cranfill. Chicago: F. H. Revell Co., 1917.

————. *Course in the English Bible.* Waco, Texas: Kellner Printing Co., n.d.

————. *Daniel and the Inter-Biblical Period.* Edited by J. B. Cranfill. Chicago: F. H. Revell Co., 1915.

————. *The Day of the Lord.* Compiled by J. W. Crowder. Edited by J. B. Cranfill. Nashville: Broadman Press, 1936.

————. *Ecclesia — The Church.* Louisville: Baptist Book, 1903.

————. *Evangelistic Sermons.* Compiled by J. B. Cranfill. Chicago: F. H. Revell Co., 1913.

————. *The Faith That Saves.* Compiled by J. W. Crowder. Edited by J. B. Cranfill. Dallas: Helms Printing Co., 1939.

————. *The Four Gospels.* Edited by J. B. Cranfill. Chicago: F. H. Revell Co., 1916.

————. *Galatians, Romans, Philippians, Philemon.* Edited by J. B. Cranfill. Chicago: F. H. Revell Co., 1916.

————. *The Hebrew Monarchy.* Edited by J. B. Cranfill. Chicago: F. H. Revell Co., 1916.

————. *The Holy Spirit.* Compiled by J. W. Crowder. Edited by J. B. Cranfill. Grand Rapids: Zondervan Publishing House, 1939.

————. *Inspiration of the Bible.* Compiled and edited by J. B. Cranfill. Chicago: F. H. Revell Co., 1930.

————. *An Interpretation of the English Bible.* Nashville: Broadman Press, 1943.

————. *James, I and II Thessalonians and I and II Corinthians.* Edited by J. B. Cranfill. Chicago: F. H. Revell Co., 1916.

————. *Jesus the Christ.* Compiled by J. W. Crowder. Edited by J. B. Cranfill. Nashville: Baird-Ward Press, 1937.

————. *Messages on Prayer.* Compiled by J. W. Crowder. Edited by J. B. Cranfill. Nashville: Broadman Press, 1942.

————. *Nature and Person of Our Lord.* Nashville: Baptist Sunday School Board, 1908.

———. *An Office Magnified.* Philadelphia: American Baptist Publication Society, 1898.

———. *Opening of the Course in the English Bible.* Waco: Kellner Printing Co., n.d.

———. *Papal Fields.* Waco: Baptist Standard Print, 1893.

———. *The Pastoral Epistles of Paul and I and II Peter, Jude, and I, II, and III John.* Edited by J. B. Cranfill. Chicago: F. H. Revell Co., 1915.

———. *Patriotism and Prohibition.* Compiled and edited by J. W. Crowder. Fort Worth, 1952.

———. *The Prophets of the Assyrian Period.* Edited by J. B. Cranfill. Chicago: F. H. Revell Co., 1917.

———. *The Providence of God.* Compiled by J. W. Crowder. Edited by J. B. Cranfill. Dallas: Helms Printing Co., 1940.

———. *Revelation.* Edited by J. B. Cranfill. Chicago: F. H. Revell Co., 1917.

———. *Revival Messages.* Compiled by J. W. Crowder. Edited by J. B. Cranfill. Grand Rapids: Zondervan Publishing House, 1939.

———. *The River of Life.* Nashville, 1928.

———. *Saved to Serve.* Compiled by J. W. Crowder. Edited by J. B. Cranfill. Dallas: Helms Printing Co., 1941.

———. *Sermons and Life Sketch of B. H. Carroll.* Compiled by J. B. Cranfill. Philadelphia: American Baptist Publication Society, 1893.

———. *Studies in Genesis.* Nashville: Broadman Press, 1937.

———. *Studies in Romans.* Nashville: Sunday School Board, 1935.

———. *Studies in Romans, Ephesians and Colossians.* Nashville: Broadman Press, 1936.

———. *The Supper and Suffering of Our Lord.* Compiled and edited by J. W. Crowder. Fort Worth, 1947.

———. *The Ten Commandments.* Nashville: Broadman Press, 1938.

———. *The Theology of the Bible.* Fort Worth: Southwestern Baptist Theological Seminary, n.d.

———. *The Way of the Cross.* Compiled by J. W. Crowder. Edited by J. B. Cranfill. Dallas: Helms Printing Co., 1941.

Carroll, J. M. "The Story of My Life, Chapters One Through Sixteen." *Journal of Texas Baptist History* 6 (1986): 37–105.

Cranfill, J. B. *J. B. Cranfill's Chronicle.* Chicago: F. H. Revell Co., 1916.

———. *B. H. Carroll and His Books.* Nashville: Broadman Press, n.d.

Dayton, A. C. *Theodosia Ernest.* Vol. 2. Philadelphia: American Baptist Publication Society, n.d.

Graves, J. R. *The New Great Iron Wheel.* N.p., n.d.

———. *Old Landmarkism: What Is It?.* 2d ed. Texarkana: Baptist Sunday School Committee, 1928.

———. *The Work of Christ Consummated in Seven Dispensations.* Memphis: J. R. Graves & Sons, 1883.

The Hayden-Cranfill Conspiracy Trial. Dallas: Texas Baptist Publishing House, 1907.

Hayden, S. A. *The Complete Conspiracy Trial Book.* Dallas: Texas Baptist Publishing House, 1907.

Jones, J. Williams. *Christ in the Camp.* Atlanta: Martin & Hoyt Co., 1904.

Martin, M. T. *Theological and Doctrinal Views of M. T. Martin.* Atlanta: Gress and Sexton, n.d.

————. "Motive and Aims." *The Gospel Standard,* January 1888.

Morrell, Z. N. *Flowers and Fruits in the Wilderness.* St. Louis: Commercial Printing Co., 1892.

Pendleton, J. M. *Christian Doctrines: A Compendium of Theology.* Philadelphia: American Baptist Publication Society, 1878.

Sampey, John R. *Memoirs of John R. Sampey.* Nashville: Broadman Press, 1947.

Whitsitt, William H. *A Question in Baptist History.* Louisville: Charles Dearing, 1896.

Unpublished Materials

Barnes, W. W. The W. W. Barnes Collection. Archives, A. Webb Roberts Library, Southwestern Baptist Theological Seminary, Fort Worth.

Carroll, B. H. The B. H. Carroll Colection. Archives, A. Webb Roberts Library, Southwestern Baptist Theological Seminary, Fort Worth.

————. "Addresses, Articles and Reports." Compiled by J. W. Crowder. Unpublished manuscript, 1939. A. Webb Roberts Library, Southwestern Baptist Theological Seminary, Fort Worth.

————. "Biblical Addresses." Compiled by J. W. Crowder. TMs, 1958, Fort Worth.

————. "Christian Education and Some Social Problems," and "The Law and the Gospel or Sin and Salvation." Compiled by J. W. Crowder. Unpublished manuscript, 1932. A. Webb Roberts Library, Southwestern Baptist Theological Seminary, Fort Worth.

————. "Controversies." Compiled by J. W. Crowder. Unpublished manuscript, 1940. A. Webb Roberts Library, Southwestern Baptist Theological Seminary, Fort Worth.

————. "The Davilla Debate Between Dr. B. H. Carroll and Dr. O. Fisher, Beginning September 13, 1871." Compiled by J. W. Crowder. Unpublished manuscript. n.d. A. Webb Roberts Library, Southwestern Baptist Theological Seminary, Fort Worth.

————. "Defending the Faith and Practices of Baptists." Compiled by J. W. Crowder. TMs, 1957. Fort Worth.

————. "Divided Kingdom." Compiled by J. W. Crowder. TMs, n.d. Fort Worth.

————. "Faith and the Faithful." Compiled by J. W. Crowder. TMs, n.d. Fort Worth.

————. "The Holy Spirit," and "Life and Its Obligations." Compiled by J. W. Crowder. Unpublished manuscript, 1932. A. Webb Roberts Library, Southwestern Baptist Theological Seminary, Fort Worth.

————. "Jesus, the Christ," and "God and His Church." Compiled by J. W. Crowder. Unpublished manuscript, 1932. A. Webb Roberts Library, Southwestern Baptist Theological Seminary, Fort Worth.

————. "Memorials, Meetings and Miscellanies." Compiled by J. W. Crowder. Unpublished manuscript, n.d. A. Webb Roberts Library, Southwestern Baptist Theological Seminary, Fort Worth.

————. "Our Seminary or the Southwestern Baptist Theological Seminary." Compiled by J. W. Crowder. TMs, 1957, Fort Worth.

————. "Our Texas Schools and Christian Education." Compiled by J. W. Crowder. Unpublished manuscript, n.d. A. Webb Roberts Library, Southwestern Baptist Theological Seminary, Fort Worth.

————. "Papal Fields." Address before the Southern Baptist Convention, Waco, Texas, 13 May 1883. A. Webb Roberts Library, Southwestern Baptist Theological Seminary, Fort Worth.

————. "Poetical Books of the Bible." Compiled by J. W. Crowder. TMs, 1957. Fort Worth.

————. "Prohibition." Sermon delivered in Waco, Texas, 30 August n.d. A. Webb Roberts Library, Southwestern Baptist Theological Seminary, Fort Worth.

————. "The Providence of God and the Christian Life," and "The Supper and Suffering of Our Lord." Compiled by J. W. Crowder. Unpublished manuscript, 1933. A. Webb Roberts Library, Southwestern Baptist Theological Seminary, Fort Worth.

————. "The Prophets of the Assyrian Period." Compiled by J. W. Crowder. Mimeographed, n.d. Fort Worth.

————. "Rivers of Living Water." Sermon delivered in Waco, Texas, 3 March 1895. A. Webb Roberts Library, Southwestern Baptist Theological Seminary, Fort Worth.

————. "The Second Advent of Christ and Final Destinies," and "Prayer and the Christian Warfare." Compiled by J. W. Crowder. Unpublished manuscript, 1933. A. Webb Roberts Library, Southwestern Baptist Theological Seminary, Fort Worth.

————. "Stewardship and Missions," and "Revival Messages." Compiled by J. W. Crowder. Unpublished manuscript, 1933. A. Webb Roberts Library, Southwestern Baptist Theological Seminary, Fort Worth.

Carroll, J. M. The J. M. Carroll Collection. Archives, A. Webb Roberts Library, Southwestern Baptist Theological Seminary, Fort Worth.

Civil Minutes of Burleson County, Book C. Burleson, Texas.

Dragan, E. C. The E. C. Dragan Papers. Southern Baptist Archives and Library, Baptist Building, Nashville.

Eaton, T. T. The T. T. Eaton Papers. Southern Baptist Archives and Library, Baptist Building, Nashville.

First Baptist Church Minutes, Books A–D. Waco, Texas.

Fort Worth Star-Telegram Scrapbook Concerning Seminary's Move to Fort Worth. Archives, A. Webb Roberts Library, Southwestern Baptist Theological Seminary, Fort Worth.

Minutes of the Baptist General Association of Texas, 1870–1886.

Minutes of the Baptist State Convention of Texas, 1870–1886.

Minutes of the Board of Trustees, 1895–1908, Baylor University. Waco, Texas.

Minutes of the Board of Trustees, 1895–1900, Southern Baptist Theological Seminary, Louisville.

Minutes of the Board of Trustees, 1907–1920, Southwestern Baptist Theological Seminary, Fort Worth.

Minutes of the First Baptist Church of Caldwell, 1866–1870. Caldwell, Texas.

Minutes of the Little River Baptist Association, 1857–1861.

Minutes of the Waco Baptist Association, 1871–1914.

Proceedings of the Baptist General Convention of Texas, 1886–1914.

Scarborough, L. R. "Certain Facts Concerning the History of Southwestern." Unpublished manuscript, n.d. Archives, A. Webb Roberts Library, Southwestern Baptist Theological Seminary, Fort Worth, 1934.

———. Lee Rutland Scarborough Papers. Archives, A. Webb Roberts Library, Southwestern Baptist Theological Seminary, Fort Worth.

Southern Baptist Convention Annual, 1896–1899.

Southwestern Baptist Theological Seminary History File. Archives, A. Webb Roberts Library, Southwestern Baptist Theological Seminary, Fort Worth.

Truett, George W. The George W. Truett Collection. Archives, A. Webb Roberts Library, Southwestern Baptist Theological Seminary, Fort Worth.

Newspapers

Baptist Argus. 1897–1908.
Baptist News. 1888–1889.
Baptist Standard. 1896–1915.
Dallas Morning News. 1885–1887.
Fort Worth Star-Telegram. 1909–1915.
Galveston Daily News. 1885–1887.
Iconoclast. 1895–1897.
Religious Herald. 1896–1898.

Texas Baptist. 1876–1886.
Texas Baptist and Herald. 1886–1900.
Texas Baptist Herald. 1860–1886.
Texas Baptist Standard. 1893–1898.
Waco Daily Examiner. 1880–1890.
Waco Day. 1885–1887.
Western Recorder. 1895–1899.

SECONDARY SOURCES

Published Materials

Baker, Robert A. *The Blossoming Desert.* Waco,Texas: Word Books, 1970.
——. *Tell the Generations Following.* Nashville: Broadman Press, 1983.
——. *The Southern Baptist Convention and Its People: 1607–1972.* Nashville: Broadman Press, 1974.
Barnes, W. W. *The Southern Baptist Convention, 1845–1953.* Nashville: Broadman Press, 1954.
Burkhalter, F. E. *A World-Visioned Church.* Nashville: Broadman Press, 1946.
Carroll, J. M. *Dr. B. H. Carroll, The Colossus of Baptist History.* Compiled and edited by J. W. Crowder. Fort Worth: By the author, 1946.
——. *A History of Texas Baptists.* Edited by J. B. Cranfill. Dallas: Baptist Standard Publishing Co., 1923.
Carver, Charles. *Brann and the Iconoclast.* Austin: University of Texas Press, 1957.
Carver, W. O. "William Heth Whitsitt: The Seminary's First Martyr." *Review and Expositor* 51 (October 1954): 449–469.
Cranfill, J. B. *B. H. Carroll and His Books.* Nashville: Broadman Press, 1943.
——. *Sermons and Life Sketch of B. H. Carroll.* Philadelphia, 1895.
Dawson, J. M. "Founder's Day Address." *Southwestern Evangel,* April 1927, 270.
Elliott, L. R., ed. *Centennial Story of Texas Baptists.* Chicago: Hammond Press, 1936.
Encyclopedia of Southern Baptists, 1958 ed. S.v. "Southwestern Baptist Theological Seminary," by W. W. Barnes.
"First Baptist Church Celebrating 125 Years." *Waco Tribune-Herald,* 2 May 1976, sec. 3, p. 1.
Harrison, Helen Bagby. *The Bagbys of Brazil.* Crawford, Texas: Crawford Christian Press, n.d.
History of First Baptist Church Caldwell, Texas. Archives, A. Webb Roberts Library, Southwestern Baptist Theological Seminary, Fort Worth.

James, Powhatan W. *George W. Truett: A Biography.* Nashville: Broadman Press, 1939.

Kelley, Dayton, ed. *Handbook of Waco and McLennan County, Texas.* Waco, Texas: Texian Press, 1972. S.v. "Baptists in McLennan County."

Kennedy, Frances, ed. *The Civil War Battlefield Guide.* Boston: Houghton Mifflin Co., 1990.

McDaniel, George White. *A Memorial Wreath.* Dallas: Baptist Standard Publishing Co., 1921.

McPherson, James M. *Battle Cry of Freedom.* New York: Oxford University Press, 1988.

Martin, T. T. *The New Testament Church.* 3d ed. Kansas City: Western Baptist Publishing Co., 1921.

Mueller, William A. *A History of Southern Baptist Theological Seminary.* Nashville: Broadman Press, 1959.

Norton, Herman. *Rebel Religion.* St. Louis: Bethany Press, n.d.

Pollard, E. B. "The Life and Work of William Heth Whitsitt." *Review and Expositor* 9 (April 1912): 159–184.

Ray, Jeff D. *B. H. Carroll.* Nashville: Sunday School Board, 1927.

Scarborough, L. R. *A Modern School of the Prophets.* Nashville: Broadman Press, 1939.

Sleeper, John, and J. C. Hutchins, comps. *Waco and McLennan County, Texas.* Waco, 1876; reprint, Waco, Texas: Texian Press, 1966.

Walker, J. L., and C. P. Lumpkin. *History of the Waco Baptist Association of Texas.* Waco, Texas: Byrne-Hill Printing House, 1897.

Weaver, Rufus W. "The Life and Times of William Heth Whitsitt." *Review and Expositor* 37 (April 1940): 113–122.

Webb, Walter Prescott, ed. *Handbook of Texas.* Austin: Texas State Historical Association, 1952. S.v. "Waco, Texas," by Roger N. Conger.

Wood, Presnall, and Floyd W. Thatcher. *Prophets with Pens: A History of the Baptist Standard.* Dallas: Baptist Standard Publishing Co., 1969.

Unpublished Materials

Aulick, A. L. "B. H. Carroll — Promoter of Christian Education." Founder's Day address delivered at Southwestern Baptist Theological Seminary in Fort Worth in 1941. Archives, A. Webb Roberts Library, Southwestern Baptist Theological Seminary, Fort Worth.

Barnes, W. W. "Founder's Day Message." Address delivered at Southwestern Baptist Theological Seminary in Fort Worth on 14 March 1957. Archives, A. Webb Roberts Library, Southwestern Baptist Theological Seminary, Fort Worth.

Boone, Joseph P. "Founder's Day Address on B. H. Carroll." Address delivered at Southwestern Baptist Theological Seminary in Fort Worth in 1955. Archives, A. Webb Roberts Library, Southwestern Baptist Theological Seminary, Fort Worth.

Bruner, James. "Dr. B. H. Carroll's Money Creed." Founder's Day address delivered at Southwestern Baptist Theological Seminary in Fort Worth in 1942. Archives, A. Webb Roberts Library, Southwestern Baptist Theological Seminary, Fort Worth.

Burroughs, Prince E. "Founder's Day Address." Address delivered at Southwestern Baptist Theological Seminary in Fort Worth on 14 March 1935. Archives, A. Webb Roberts Library, Southwestern Baptist Theological Seminary, Fort Worth.

Dawson, J. M. "B. H. Carroll and Baylor University." Address delivered to the Baylor Historical Society in Waco, Texas, on 21 April 1958. Archives, A. Webb Roberts Library, Southwestern Baptist Theological Seminary, Fort Worth.

Evans, Perry. "Founder's Day Address." Address delivered at Southwestern Baptist Theological Seminary in Fort Worth in 1953. Archives, A. Webb Roberts Library, Southwestern Baptist Theological Seminary, Fort Worth.

Ray, Jeff D. "The First Faculty of the Seminary." Founder's Day address delivered at Southwestern Baptist Theological Seminary in Fort Worth in 1948. Archives, A. Webb Roberts Library, Southwestern Baptist Theological Seminary, Fort Worth.

Williams, Charles B. "B. H. Carroll: The Titanic Interpreter and Teacher of Truth." TMs, n.d. A. Webb Roberts Library, Southwestern Baptist Theological Seminary, Fort Worth.

Theses and Dissertations

Beck, Rosalie. "The Whitsitt Controversy: A Denomination in Crisis." Ph.D. diss., Baylor University, 1985.

Bugg, Charles Basil. "The Whitsitt Controversy: A Study in Denominational Conflict." Ph.D. diss., Southern Baptist Theological Seminary, 1972.

Cates, J. Dee. "B. H. Carroll: The Man and His Ethics." Th.D. diss., Southwestern Baptist Theological Seminary, 1962.

Cogburn, Keith. "B. H. Carroll and Controversy." M.A. thesis, Baylor University, 1983.

Leddon, James A. "Texas Baptists and the Whitsitt Controversy." M.A. thesis, Texas Western College, 1964.

Robinson, Robert Jackson. "The Homiletical Method of Benajah Harvey Carroll." Th.D. diss., Southwestern Baptist Theological Seminary, 1956.

Stewart, Wilson Lannin. "Ecclesia: The Motif of B. H. Carroll's Theology." Th.D. diss., Southwestern Baptist Theological Seminary, 1959.

Tull, James E. "A Study of Southern Baptist Landmarkism in the Light of Historical Baptist Ecclesiology." Ph.D. diss., Columbia University, 1960.

Watson, Tom L. "The Eschatology of B. H. Carroll." M.Th. thesis, Southwestern Baptist Theological Seminary, 1960.

Index

tism of, 19; began teaching, 17;
William C. Brann Controversy,
57; Carroll-Compere Controversy, 34; chairman of Exegesis &
Systematic Theology at Baylor,
82; children of 21; Confederate
service, 13–16; consolidation of
Baptist General Association and
Baptist Convention, 52; dean of
Bible Department at Baylor, 96;
death of, 122; death of father, 15;
debate with Fisher, 27; "Defender
of Faith," 27–28, divorces first
wife Ophelia A. Crunck, 14; early
life of, 2, 8; education of, 9, 12;
family of, 1–7; feeble health of,
29; final years of, 118; financial
difficulties of, 22; first contact
with Waco University, 32; first
report of Baylor Theological Seminary, 101; S. A. Hayden Controversy, 57, 68–73; injury of, 16–17;
intellect of, 43–44; marries first
wife Ophelia A. Crunck, 14; marries second wife Ellen Bell, 20;
Methodist Camp Meeting, 18;
M. T. Martin Controversy, 62–68;
music in ceremony, 28; newspaper controversy, 36, 38; pastor
Caldwell Baptist Church, 79; pastor First Baptist, Waco, 25–26, 39,
75–82; pastor New Hope Baptist
Church, 23, 25; pastor Post Oak
Baptist Church, 22, 24; philosophy of preaching, 40–42; physical
description, 42–43; president of
Southwestern Baptist Theological
Seminary, 105; principal of Bible
Department at Baylor, 84; prohibition, 30–32, 45–51; religious life
of, 7–9; resignation from Board of
Trustees at Baylor, 105; resignation from Chairman of Mission
Board, 57; resignation from Education Commission, 97; resignation from First Baptist, Waco, 30,
78, 94; second wife Ellen Bell
dies, 77; skepticism of Christian-

ity, 8–9; third wife Hallie Harri-
son caring for, 121; William Heth
Whittsitt Controversy, 86–90
Carroll, Benajah, 1–2, 4–7
  Ellen Bell, 20, 77
  Guy, 118
  Hallie Harrison, 121
  J. M., 1, 14, 18, 25, 50, 69–70, 78, 94
  Jesse, 2
  Laban, 16
  Mary Eliza, 1–2, 7
Carroll-Compere Controversy, 34
Carver, W. O., 84
Central Baptist Educational Commis-
  sion, 32
Centralization, 71
City Market Opera House, 30
Cogburn, Keith, 35, 57, 90
Coke, Senator Richard, 45–50
Columbus Avenue Baptist Church, 75
Compere, Thomas H., 34
Confederate Army, 13–16
Connell, G. H., 120
Coulson, G. A., 92
Cranfill, J. B., 14, 48–49, 68–69, 72,
  94, 122, 127
Crawford, T. P., 70
Crittenden, T. K., 12
Crowder, J. W., 34, 94, 118, 127
Crunk, Ophelia A., 14

D
Dayton, A. C., 74
Democratic Party, 45
Dove Baptist Church, 4

E
East Texas Baptist Convention, 35
Eaton, T. T., 77
Education Commission, 78, 94, 97
Evans, B. D., 14

F
Finley, N. W., 50
First Baptist, Belton, 38
First Baptist, Dallas, 34, 71, 105
First Baptist, Fort Worth, 120
First Baptist, Marlin, 67
First Baptist, San Antonio, 30
First Baptist, Waco, 23–32, 38–40, 48,
  56, 64, 71, 75–82, 94, 124, 125

Pierson, M. S., 58
Pool, W. A., 110
Post Oak Church, 22
Prohibition Democrats, 32
Prohibition Movement, 4, 30, 39, 45–
  51, 50, 124, 125

Q
Question in Baptist History, A, 87

R
Ray, Jeff D., 14, 21, 26, 32, 42, 61, 81,
  94, 104–105, 122
"Real Issue in the Whitsitt Case, The,"
  90
Reeves, Professor J. J., 121
Religious Herald, 122
Richland Association, 34
Robertson, A. T., 87, 91, 93

S
Sampey, John R., 40, 62, 87, 91, 101
Scarborough, L. R., 117, 118, 122, 126
Schneider, H. William, 50
Seventh and James Baptist Church, 75
Smith, M. V., 36–38, 68
Southern Baptist Convention, 36, 38,
  51, 59, 121–122, 124, 126
Southern Baptist Convention Minutes,
  36
Southern Baptist Theological Semi-
  nary, 62, 93
Southern Seminary, 21, 91
Southern Seminary in Louisville, 126
Southwestern Baptist Theological
  Seminary, 105–117, 123, 125
Sparks, S. F., 76
Spring Hill Church, 22
State Convention, 35
State Prohibition Alliance, 48
Stephens, Alexander, 93
Sunday School Board, 61, 123

T
Tanner, John, 97
  John S., 84

Texas Baptist, 36, 53
Texas Baptist Herald, 23, 26, 27, 28–
  29, 31, 34–35, 36, 38, 53, 62, 79
Texas Baptist and Herald, 54, 58, 64,
  65, 68–72
Texas Baptist Standard, 68
Texas Prohibition Party, 48, 50
Texas Rangers, 12–14
Texas Resolution of October 1896, 88
Theological Department of Baylor,
  96–99
Touchstone, J. R. M., 67
Truett, George W., 55, 71, 82, 112, 122
Tucker, H. H., 67
Tull, James, 91

U
United Friends of Temperance, The,
  45
University of Chicago, 84

W
Waco Advance, 48, 49, 68
Waco Association Minutes, 33
Waco Baptist Association, 51, 67–68
Waco Classical School, 23
Waco Examiner, 45
Waco Suspension Bridge, 24
Waco University, 23, 32, 52, 82, 125
Walker, J. L., 51
Western Baptist, 68–69
Western Recorder, 122
Whitsitt, William Heth, 84–94, 111,
  123
"Whitsitt Case at Wilmington, The,"
  90
Whitsitt Controversy, W. H., 60, 62,
  72, 75, 84–94, 96, 99, 110, 111,
  123, 124, 125
Williams, C. B., 42, 44, 97
  Roger, 85

Y
Yellow Prairie, 17

About the Author

Alan J. Lefever has served as the director of the Texas Baptist Historical Collection since 1991 and is also currently an adjunct professor of Church History at Truett Seminary at Baylor University. A native of Maryland, he was raised in San Antonio, Texas. He earned his B.A. from Baylor University and his M.Div. and Ph.D. from Southwestern Seminary. During his study at Southwestern he received the Robert A. Baker Award in Church History. He also holds a Certificate of Archival Administration from the University of Texas at Arlington. Lefever has also served as the archivist at Southwestern and on the staff of four churches in Texas and has been a guest preacher in churches throughout the South.

As Archivist, he oversees the Texas Baptist Historical Collection and is active in the Texas Baptist Historical Society. He has authored numerous articles dealing with Texas Baptists and is a specialist in the area of Texas Baptist history. His most recent book A History of Baylor Sports was released in 2013.

www.ingramcontent.com/pod-product-compliance
Lightning Source LLC
Chambersburg PA
CBHW060049100426
42742CB00014B/2754